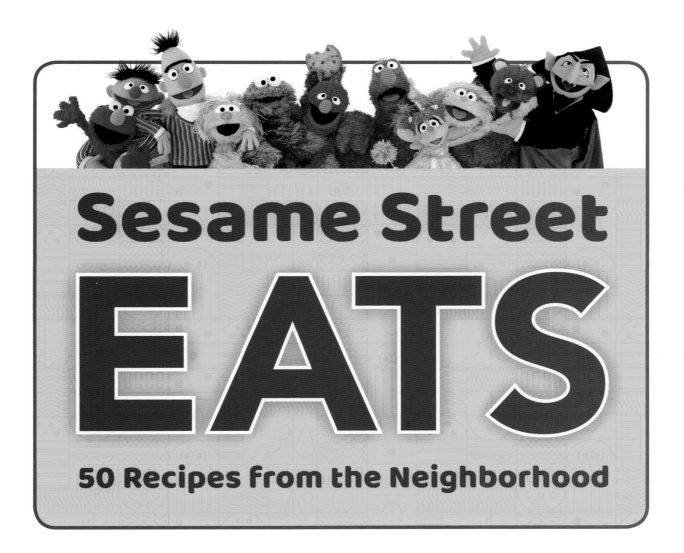

Sesame Street
EATS
50 Recipes from the Neighborhood

STERLING CHILDREN'S BOOKS
New York

STERLING CHILDREN'S BOOKS
New York

An Imprint of Sterling Publishing Co., Inc.
1166 Avenue of the Americas
New York, NY 10036

ISBN 978-1-4549-3511-7

Distributed in Canada by Sterling Publishing Co., Inc.
c/o Canadian Manda Group, 664 Annette Street
Toronto, Ontario M6S 2C8, Canada

For information about custom editions, special sales, and premium
and corporate purchases, please contact Sterling Special Sales at
800-805-5489 or specialsales@sterlingpublishing.com.

Manufactured in China

Lot #:
2 4 6 8 10 9 7 5 3 1
06/19

sterlingpublishing.com

Edited and designed by Girl Friday Productions
See page 128 for image credits.

Contents

Cooking with *Sesame Street*

If you want a bite to eat on Sesame Street, try Mr. Hooper's Store. The grocery store and diner was a beloved part of the original world of *Sesame Street*, a place for characters to gather and show kids that healthy food is a central part of a community. Although ownership of the store has changed over time, its role as a place to meet on the street has stayed the same. That's because on Sesame Street, just like in neighborhoods the world over, food brings family and friends together.

Cooking has always been an important way to learn on *Sesame Street*. Cookie Monster knows the difference between healthy, everyday foods—like fruits and vegetables—and sometimes foods—like his beloved cookies. Super Grover and super foods make a great pair. Ernie loves breakfast. And vegetables are always something to sing about.

The fun doesn't stop on the street—everywhere they go, the *Sesame Street* characters try to learn about new flavors and cuisines.

Join *Sesame Street* for 50 recipes that celebrate 50 years of trying, tasting, learning, and growing. Each time kids get to help in the kitchen, they learn about good food—and everything that goes into making it. So get cooking, and enjoy!

Cooking with Kids

What is a kitchen? For starters, it's a laboratory for science and mathematics. It's a library filled with stories and new words. It's a colorful art studio. It's a ticket to travel the world and learn about other cultures. It's a place where real work happens and where creativity takes center stage. Best of all, it's a place where parents and kids can come together and learn from one another, and have fun!

When kids cook and eat with their parents, they learn about making healthy choices. They get to experiment with delicious new foods. They experience the magical transformation of ingredients into a finished dish to share with those they love. Getting kids excited about cooking from a young age will change the way they think about food. By making and eating wholesome foods and dishes alongside your kids, you teach them that being healthy can be both fun and delicious.

Cooking and sharing meals with your kids also gives them the confidence that comes from doing an important job. Helping to feed the family is a big deal! And just wait until you see your kids' proud faces when they're putting the food they made on the table. It's a powerful feeling.

With kids in the kitchen, things might take a little longer and get a little messier than when you're cooking alone. And chances are the finished dish isn't going to look perfect. What do you get instead? Tremendous fun with your kids.

As you're cooking, let kids help with age-appropriate tasks (see p. 7 for ideas). As you cook together, let them smell spices, touch ingredients (after washing hands), and sample uncooked and cooked veggies to taste the difference. They'll develop new vocabulary as they learn to describe what they're cooking and eating.

When you can, work with kids to plan recipes for the week. Let them watch you making a grocery list, checking the pantry and refrigerator, then writing out the items to get at the store. If your children are reading and writing, they can help make the list. Younger children can add check boxes to your list. Taking children to the grocery store can be a learning adventure, too. Put them in charge of picking out pieces of produce you'll use, or ask them to help find ingredients.

Cleanup is part of cooking, too, and it's a responsibility kids will gladly take on. Talk to them about how they clean up their toys, and explain that the same thing happens after you cook. Discuss with them how you organize the kitchen—where do pots and pans go? Let them help you put them away.

And of course a big part of cooking is sharing the dish with your family. As much as possible, try to remember to put away electronics and focus on being together during mealtimes. Ask questions, play games, taste-test foods, and enjoy one another's company.

In These Pages

This book contains 50 unique, kid-friendly recipes—one for every year that *Sesame Street* has been on the air so far!

Each recipe includes a list of ingredients and equipment, so you and your child can gather what you need together before you begin cooking. Throughout, **SLIMEY'S SUGGESTION!** boxes highlight substitutions, serving suggestions, and variations to try. **TWIDDLEBUG**

TIPs help direct parents to ways their kids can help with each recipe or engage with the cooking process to learn new things. Kids can flip through the pages to find their favorite *Sesame Street* characters—they pop up in every recipe, offering opportunities to learn, laugh, and think.

The book closes with **TOGETHER TIME** (see p. 122), a section with ideas to make the most of your family time in the kitchen and at the table.

Kid-Friendly and Kid-Fun Recipes

The recipes in *Sesame Street Eats* were created with your kids in mind. The instructions are written for adults to follow, but every recipe contains something a child can do or help you with, depending on the child's age and skill level (see p. 7 for ideas).

Before you begin cooking, check your recipe's equipment list. You may require child-friendly equipment, like measuring cups and measuring spoons, child-sized aprons, and plastic serrated knives for cutting soft foods. Then arrange your child's work space with these tools when prepping your kitchen.

MAKE RECIPES INTERACTIVE: Fun with kids in the kitchen can start before you even begin cooking. Reading recipes with children gets them excited to cook!

1. Read the recipe out loud before you start cooking. Even if you know a recipe well, reading it with your child allows you to plan and prepare together. Pick out the steps you feel comfortable allowing your children to do on their own.
2. As you read through the ingredients and equipment, kids can help gather what you'll need.
3. Ask children to find numbers or favorite letters from the recipe.
4. Talk about fractions by showing them that two half cups of water fit perfectly into one whole cup. You can also cut a round fruit in half and show how two halves make a whole. Cut it in half again to talk about quarters.

Kids Can Help in the Kitchen!

EVERY CHILD IS DIFFERENT. Follow your instincts when cooking with your children. Children will be ready for different tasks at different times. These guidelines represent tasks that an average child of each age can help with.

Children younger than four can try:
- Wiping down your counters before and after cooking
- Rinsing and draining canned or frozen ingredients, such as the corn kernels for Rosita's Calypso Corn Muffins (see p. 16)
- Sprinkling cheese over Snuffleupagus's Loaded-Up Potato Skins (see p. 40)
- Stirring or whisking ingredients together, such as the dry ingredients in Oscar's Monster Muffins (see p. 32)
- Snapping the ends off green beans for Bert & Ernie's Slightly Nutty Green Beans (see p. 64)
- Smashing cucumbers with a rolling pin for Grover's Crushed Cucumber Salad (see p. 72)
- Rinsing fresh fruit, such as the berries for Telly Monster's Any-Berry Crisp (see p. 104)

Children older than four can do all the tasks younger children can do, as well as:
- Measuring dry ingredients, such as those in Cookie Monster's Everything Cookie (see p. 102)
- Mashing soft foods, like the egg in Elmo's Egg in a Blanket (see p. 22)

- Peeling a banana, such as for Bert & Ernie's Best Buddies Banana Pancakes (see p. 18), or carefully peeling a hard-boiled egg for Elmo's Egg in a Blanket (see p. 22)
- Cracking an egg into a bowl, to make Abby Cadabby's Pink Fairy Cakes (see p. 108)—have some extra eggs ready just in case!
- Helping set and clear the table
- Putting away ingredients that belong in easy-to-reach places

REMEMBER: Children must be supervised at all times in the kitchen, even when working on an age-appropriate task. Read Abby Cadabby's list of kitchen safety rules (see p. 9) aloud to children before you begin.

Notes on Ingredients

When adapting any recipe to fit your family's needs, keep these nutrition ideas in mind:

- **WHOLE GRAINS:** When possible, health experts recommend cooking with and eating whole grains, like whole-wheat flour, brown rice, and whole-grain breads.
- **LOW-FAT DAIRY:** The recipes in this book use low-fat milk and dairy, and low-fat or nonfat yogurt. The American Academy of Pediatrics and the American Heart Association recommend low-fat dairy products for children two years and older. Low-fat dairy products pack all the same nutrients as full-fat dairy.
- **FRUITS AND VEGETABLES:** Serve up extra helpings of fruits and vegetables alongside the recipes in *Sesame Street Eats*. Challenge your children (and other family members) to make half of each plate fruits and veggies for plenty of fiber and nutrients.

Eating Safely

- **CHOKING HAZARDS:** Make sure foods are sliced small to prevent choking. For safety, halve or quarter any round pieces of foods (for instance, grapes, cherry tomatoes, and carrots). Also chop firm foods into little pieces.
- **ALLERGIES:** According to the American Academy of Pediatrics, approximately 8 percent of children in the U.S. have been diagnosed with a food allergy. Some of the most common foods that cause allergic reactions include peanuts, tree nuts, fish, shellfish, eggs, wheat, soy, and sesame. Since food allergies are common in young children, be aware when cooking with common allergens and keep a close eye on your children. When cooking with your children and their friends, make sure to check with the friends' parents about any possible food allergies. Remember that allergic reactions vary greatly, from mild to life-threatening. If you have a child with a food allergy, avoid any recipe with ingredients that might be dangerous. It is also extremely important to check the ingredients list on all products and avoid products that don't have ingredients clearly listed on the label. Keep in mind that some foods are prepared in environments that also process allergens, like tree nuts. Finally, children under the age of one should never be given honey.

Kitchen Safety Magic with Abby Cadabby!

Abby Cadabby here! The kitchen is such a magical place. But even with a magic wand, you have to be extra careful when you're cooking. Read these safety rules aloud with a grown-up to learn how to always stay safe in the kitchen.

1. **You need company in the kitchen.** There should always be a grown-up nearby when you're cooking.

2. **You get a special place to work in the kitchen.** A grown-up should make sure your work space is away from hot stove tops, hot pots and pans, and open flames. Also, ask your grown-up to help you check around and above you to make sure nothing can fall on you and hurt you.

3. **Never ever touch anything sharp.** Only grown-ups can work with grown-up knives, food processor blades, blender blades, scissors, or any other sharp objects in the kitchen.

4. **Never ever go near anything hot.** Grown-ups are in charge of moving food into the oven and taking it out when it's ready. Only grown-ups can cook food on a hot stove top, oven, or griddle.

5. **Use only clean hands in the kitchen.** So wash your hands a lot! Use lots of soap and warm water to wash your hands carefully before you start cooking, and after you touch any raw meat or eggs, so that you don't get germs from those foods in your body or on other parts of the kitchen. Try not to put your fingers in your mouth when you're cooking—and if you do, wash them right away! If you sneeze or cough into your hands or use the bathroom, wash your hands carefully before you get back to cooking.

6. **Your work space must be sparkling clean.** The first step to cooking is cleaning! You don't want any germs to get into your meal, so make sure you wipe off your counter before you prepare food. Ask grown-ups to make sure your area is neat and ready to begin cooking.

7. **Pick up kitchen ingredients and equipment like you pick up your toys.** When you are done with an ingredient, help put away any leftovers. When you are finished with a piece of equipment, grown-ups will show you where it goes to be cleaned.

8. **Be serious about safety.** You can help keep the kitchen safe! Remind grown-ups to make sure there are no pot handles sticking out from the stove, no electric cords hanging off the counter, and no knives or sharp utensils lying around.

9. **Be careful and take it slow!** Do just one task at a time.

10. **Enjoy your food.** When it's time to eat the magical meal you made, eat slowly and chew your food well before you swallow. Bon appétit! (That means happy eating in French!)

Eat Your Colors!

Sesame Street is a colorful place! And foods come in all different colors, too. It's fun to think of foods for every color of the rainbow. Try to think of some other foods in different colors! What's a red food that you like to eat? What about orange, yellow, green, blue, purple, and pink? Are there foods you can think of that don't fit any of these colors?

Elmo likes to eat
RED tomatoes.

Zoe gobbles down
ORANGE carrots.

Big Bird likes to sip
YELLOW lentil soup.

Oscar the Grouch
eats **GREEN** kiwis.

Grover loves to eat his favorite **BLUE** blueberries in the summertime.

Me like cookies best of all, but me also like eating rainbow foods. Mmm, rainbows.

Telly Monster is a big fan of delicious **PURPLE** eggplant.

Julia likes to eat **PINK** grapefruit in the morning.

Eating your colors is fun! Try to make your plate look really colorful. Get a few different colors in every meal—sometimes you can even get a whole rainbow in every bite! Get a grown-up to help you! Here are some fun ideas for eating your colors:

- Can you keep track of all the colors you eat during the day and see how many you can get?
- Can you create a rainbow meal that includes every color?
- Can you create a meal that uses just one color? A breakfast, lunch, or dinner where everything is green? Or orange? Or red?
- At the grocery store, can you find fruits and vegetables in every color?

Are You a Food Explorer?

- Every time you try a new food, it's an adventure! Explore your food. Talk about it with a grown-up.
- What does it look like? Get up close! What color is it? What shape does it have? Do you serve it with a spoon or cut it with a knife? Do you eat it with a fork or a spoon or even your hands?
- What does it taste like? (This is called the *flavor* of the food.) Is it sweet? Spicy? Salty? Does it taste tangy or sour or bitter or buttery? Does the taste change as you're chewing?
- What does it feel like? (This is called the *texture*.) Is it crunchy or soft? Is it leafy or smooth or hard or chewy or grainy?

When you try lots of new foods, you learn to love lots of different flavors! Sometimes a food's taste or texture might surprise you. But take some time to try it again. The more times you taste new foods, the yummier you usually find them!

ELMO SAYS: Help plan your meal!

Elmo loves pictures. Every recipe in this book has a picture that goes with it. Look at the pictures. What colors do you see?

Do what Elmo does and help a grown-up pick two or three colorful recipes to serve together for a whole meal. Grown-ups can tell you about making sure you have protein, grains, fruits, and veggies on your plate.

Breakfasts for Champions

We've all heard the saying: breakfast is the most important meal of the day. And it's true! For kids especially, a healthy breakfast provides the energy needed to do all the learning, growing, and playing they'll pack into their busy day. These recipes are filled with whole grains, proteins, fruits, and vegetables to get everyone off on the right foot in the morning. And with so many great options to choose from, your family might start wanting breakfast for dinner, too!

Sunny Days
EGG & SPINACH SCRAMBLE
Makes 4 servings

This dish is a cross between scrambled eggs and a frittata, filled with lots of tasty ingredients but cooked on the stove top. No matter what you call it, kids love it.

INGREDIENTS

3 tablespoons vegetable oil
1 yellow onion, chopped
1 pound ground turkey
1 package frozen spinach, thawed
    and thoroughly drained
Salt
Tabasco or other
    hot sauce (optional)
4 eggs, lightly beaten
¼ cup grated Parmesan cheese

EQUIPMENT

Measuring spoons
Knife
Cutting board
Fork
Strainer
Measuring cups
Medium bowl
Large skillet

1 Heat the oil in a large skillet over medium heat. Add the onion, and cook until the onion is soft, about 3 minutes.

2 Add the ground turkey, breaking it up into small bits with a fork; cook until the meat is no longer pink in the center. Add the spinach and mix well. Cook, stirring, for 2–3 minutes, then add salt to taste.

3 Add a dash of Tabasco to the beaten eggs (if using), then pour the egg mixture over the meat and greens, and stir until the eggs have set, 1–2 minutes.

4 Place on a warm serving platter, sprinkle with the Parmesan cheese, and serve hot.

SLIMEY'S SUGGESTION!
Ground chicken or lean beef can be substituted for the turkey. Or skip the meat altogether for a vegetarian scramble.

Rosita's
CALYPSO CORN MUFFINS
Makes 12 muffins

These delicious muffins make a hearty, healthy breakfast—especially when served alongside some scrambled eggs and fresh fruit! They also serve as a wonderful accompaniment to Count's Chili with Three Beans (see p. 78), Elmo's Red Lentil Soup (see p. 86), or any other warming soup or stew.

INGREDIENTS
6 tablespoons unsalted butter, melted, plus extra for greasing muffin tin
1¼ cups stone-ground yellow cornmeal
¾ cup all-purpose flour
⅓ cup granulated sugar
1 tablespoon baking powder
¼ teaspoon baking soda
¼ teaspoon salt
1 egg
⅔ cup buttermilk
⅓ cup finely diced pimiento pepper
1 cup frozen corn kernels, thawed
1 (4-ounce) can mild diced green chilies (optional)

EQUIPMENT
Measuring cups
Measuring spoons
Knife
Cutting board
12-cup standard-size muffin tin
Large mixing bowl
Small mixing bowl
Whisk
Strainer
Wooden spoon
Cooling rack

1 Preheat the oven to 400°F. Lightly grease a 12-cup muffin tin with melted butter.

2 In a large mixing bowl, combine the cornmeal, flour, sugar, baking powder, baking soda, and salt. In a small bowl, beat the egg thoroughly, then whisk in the buttermilk.

3 Place the peppers in a strainer and rinse them thoroughly with cold water. Add the corn to the strainer—as well as the green chilies, if using—and press hard with the back of a wooden spoon to extract as much moisture as possible.

4 Add the pepper-corn mixture to the buttermilk mixture and stir to combine. Add the buttermilk mixture and the melted butter to the dry ingredients; stir until just combined.

5 Spoon the batter into the prepared muffin tin, dividing it evenly and filling the cups about three-quarters full. Place the tin on an oven rack in the middle of the oven and bake for about 35 minutes, or until the muffins are golden brown. Let cool for 10–15 minutes before removing from the tin. Serve warm.

Kids love to help bake! They can help pour measured ingredients into the bowl, stir, and grease the muffin tin. They can also try pouring the milk and cracking the eggs. If there's a spill or a mess, it's a great way to show kids that mistakes are OK. That's how we learn!

What is the most magical vegetable of them all? *The uni-corn!*

Bert & Ernie's
BEST BUDDIES BANANA PANCAKES
Makes 4 servings (about 8 pancakes)

Pancakes make a great dish for a more leisurely weekend family breakfast or brunch. Kids can measure and mix while grown-ups cook up a fun variety of shapes and sizes.

INGREDIENTS
1 (6-ounce) container plain nonfat yogurt
2 eggs
1 tablespoon unsalted butter, melted
⅔ cup all-purpose flour
⅓ cup whole-wheat flour
2 tablespoons granulated sugar or honey
2 teaspoons baking soda
¼ teaspoon cinnamon
¼ teaspoon salt
1 ripe banana, sliced
Nonfat milk (as needed)

Cooking spray, for greasing
½ cup strawberry jam or maple syrup

EQUIPMENT
Measuring spoons
Measuring cups
Large mixing bowl
Medium mixing bowl
Knife
Cutting board
Large nonstick skillet or griddle
Spatula
Small, heavy saucepan

1 In a large bowl, combine the yogurt, eggs, and melted butter. In a separate medium bowl, combine both flours and the sugar or honey, baking soda, cinnamon, and salt. Add the flour mixture to the yogurt mixture, stirring until blended. Stir in the banana. The batter should be thick, but pourable. If it is too thick, thin it out with a tablespoon or two of milk.

2 Coat a large nonstick skillet or griddle with the cooking spray and set it over high heat. When a drop of water sizzles on it, pour the batter using a quarter measuring cup. Cook until bubbles begin to appear at the edges of the pancakes, 2–3 minutes. Flip and cook until golden, 2–3 minutes longer. Repeat with the remaining batter.

3 Place the jam or syrup in a small, heavy saucepan over low heat and cook until warm. (Or place the jam in a microwavable-safe dish and microwave on high until hot, 1–1½ minutes.)

4 Serve the pancakes immediately with the warm jam or syrup.

Twiddlebug Tip Try using different fruits! If you have leftover fresh fruit, such as blueberries or apples (peeled and thinly sliced), try adding it to the pancake batter with (or instead of) the banana.

Try peeling a banana from the end away from the stem. Just pinch the end!

Baby Bear's
PORRIDGE WITH WARM APPLESAUCE

Makes 4 servings

Porridge is an old-fashioned name for oatmeal or any other warm, soft food made with cooked grains or legumes. This classic version gets its sweetness from a quick and easy homemade applesauce.

INGREDIENTS

Applesauce
2 large McIntosh, Braeburn, or red apples, peeled, cored, and chopped
1 teaspoon brown sugar
¼ teaspoon cinnamon
1 teaspoon freshly squeezed lemon juice

Oatmeal
2 cups water
2 cups nonfat milk
2 cups quick-cooking rolled oats

EQUIPMENT
Knife
Vegetable peeler
Cutting board
Measuring spoons
Measuring cups
2 medium heavy saucepans, one with a lid
Wooden spoon

1 Make the applesauce: Place the apples, brown sugar, cinnamon, and lemon juice in a heavy saucepan. Cook over medium heat, stirring constantly, until the apples soften and the sauce reaches the consistency you prefer, 15–20 minutes. If the applesauce needs more liquid, add a tablespoon or two of water or a bit more lemon juice. Remove the pan from the heat, and place the lid on to keep the applesauce warm.

2 Make the oatmeal: Combine the water and milk in a heavy saucepan and bring it to a boil. Sprinkle the oatmeal over the boiling liquid, stirring constantly to prevent lumps from forming; continue cooking until the oatmeal is the consistency you prefer, 4–5 minutes.

3 Serve hot, topped with a generous dollop of applesauce.

SLIMEY'S SUGGESTION!
Applesauce is very easy to make, and tastes delicious with pancakes, quick breads, cake, and also savory dishes, such as pork.

21

Elmo's
EGG IN A BLANKET
Makes 1 wrap

This egg salad wrap gets its zip from mustard and chopped green olives. Serve it alongside Abby Cadabby's Magical Mango & Banana Smoothie (see p. 24) or a plate of fresh fruit for a bright start to any day.

INGREDIENTS
1 egg
1–2 teaspoons low-fat mayonnaise, to taste
2 teaspoons Dijon or other mustard
3–4 pimento-stuffed green olives, finely chopped
Salt and ground black pepper
Lettuce
1 whole-wheat sandwich wrap or
    whole-wheat tortilla

EQUIPMENT
Measuring spoons
Knife
Cutting board
Saucepan
Slotted spoon
2 small bowls

1 Hard-boil the egg: Place the egg in a saucepan, cover it with water, and bring it to a rolling boil. Reduce the heat, and simmer for 12 minutes. Using a slotted spoon, transfer the egg to a small bowl of ice water to cool. When cool, peel the egg.

2 In another small bowl, mash the peeled egg, then gently mix with the mayonnaise, mustard, and chopped olives. Add salt and pepper to taste.

3 Place a lettuce leaf or two on the whole-wheat wrap. Pile the egg mixture on the lettuce, fold the sides of the wrap in toward the center, and roll the wrap up from the bottom. Cut the wrap in two crosswise, and serve.

SLIMEY'S SUGGESTION!
Make a true "veggie" wrap by using a sturdy piece of romaine or iceberg lettuce. Just pile the egg mixture on the lettuce leaf and roll it up the way you would a tortilla or other wrap.

Eggs contain vitamin D, which helps Keep your bones strong and your body healthy!

23

Abby Cadabby's
MAGICAL MANGO & BANANA SMOOTHIE

Makes about 4 (8-ounce) smoothies

Smoothies are an extra-healthy choice for breakfast or for snacks! And sweet, succulent mangoes are delicious in smoothies. If you can't find a mango, consider making your smoothie "Abby pink" by using strawberries, raspberries, or watermelon in place of the mango.

INGREDIENTS

1 mango, washed, peeled, and cut into chunks, or 1 cup frozen diced mango
2 ripe bananas, peeled and cut into chunks
1 cup nonfat milk (or substitute almond milk, coconut milk, rice milk, or nut milk of choice)
1 (6-ounce) container low-fat or nonfat vanilla yogurt

EQUIPMENT

Knife
Cutting board
Measuring cups
Blender

1 Place the mango chunks, bananas, milk, and yogurt in a blender and blend on high until smooth and creamy.

There are lots and lots of kinds of mangoes grown around the world—more than 1,000 varieties!

This simple recipe can easily be made by older children, and they'll feel proud of their cooking efforts. A grown-up should always supervise, because blenders have sharp blades. For younger kids, ask them to choose their favorite combination of fruit and yogurt!

Oscar's
GREEN MONSTER SMOOTHIE
Makes 2–4 servings

This nutty-sweet smoothie is an easy way to sneak in a whole cupful of greens, plus fiber and protein. It tastes like a milkshake for breakfast!

INGREDIENTS
1 ripe banana, peeled and cut into chunks
1 cup low-fat milk (or substitute almond milk, soy milk, rice milk, or nut milk of choice)
1 cup baby spinach leaves, washed and dried
1–2 tablespoons peanut butter (or substitute other nut butters or sunflower butter)
1 tablespoon chia seeds (optional)
3–4 ice cubes

EQUIPMENT
Knife
Cutting board
Measuring cups
Measuring spoons
Blender

1 Place all the ingredients in a blender and blend on high until smooth.

SLIMEY'S SUGGESTION!
You can use less milk to make a thicker smoothie. Or for a fun twist, dollop tablespoons of the thick smoothie on a parchment-lined baking sheet and freeze for "frozen smoothie bites"!

Julia's
CRUNCHY BAKED GRANOLA WITH YOGURT & FRUIT
Makes about 5 cups granola

This tasty granola can be made with whatever nuts and dried fruits you like and keeps in an airtight container for up to a month. Served with fresh fruit and yogurt, it's a sunny start to any day.

INGREDIENTS
⅓ cup canola oil
⅓ cup honey, maple syrup, or
    firmly packed light-brown sugar
½ teaspoon cinnamon
½ teaspoon salt
3 cups old-fashioned rolled oats (not quick-
    cooking)
1 cup chopped nuts (such as almonds, cashews,
    walnuts, or pecans)
1 cup chopped dried fruit (such as raisins,
    cranberries, apricots, or apples)
Low-fat vanilla yogurt, for serving

Fresh fruit (such as blueberries and sliced
    bananas), for serving

EQUIPMENT
Measuring cups
Measuring spoons
Knife
Cutting board
Rimmed baking sheet
Parchment paper or aluminum foil
Large mixing bowl
Whisk
Spatula
Cooling rack

1 Preheat the oven to 300°F. Line a rimmed baking sheet with parchment paper or aluminum foil.

2 In a large bowl, whisk together the oil, honey, cinnamon, and salt.

3 Add oats and chopped nuts to the oil mixture, and stir to evenly coat the dry ingredients with the oil.

4 Spread the granola mixture into an even layer on the prepared baking sheet. Press down with the back of a spatula. (This helps the granola form clumps.)

5 Bake for 20–25 minutes, stirring once halfway through, until golden brown. Remove the granola from the oven, stir in the dried fruit, press the mixture down again with the back of a spatula, and let it cool to room temperature on a rack.

6 When cool, serve the granola with vanilla yogurt and fresh fruit.

Elmo's
MUFFIN-CUP QUICHE

Makes 12 mini quiches

Mini quiches are just as cute as Elmo himself and make an extra-special breakfast. Substitute different veggies—like broccoli, mushrooms, or bell peppers—for some or all the potatoes to make the quiches even more colorful.

INGREDIENTS

Cooking spray, vegetable oil, or melted butter, for greasing
2 tablespoons olive oil
2 medium russet potatoes, diced (about 1½ cups)
½ yellow onion, diced
1 teaspoon salt
8 eggs
1 cup shredded low-fat Cheddar cheese
½ cup low-fat milk
1½ cups baby spinach leaves, washed and dried

EQUIPMENT

Measuring spoons
Knife
Cutting board
Measuring cups
12-cup standard-size muffin tin
Large skillet
Plate
Medium bowl
Whisk
Ladle

1 Preheat the oven to 325°F.

2 Coat a 12-cup muffin tin with cooking spray, or rub the inside of each cup with oil or melted butter.

3 Heat the olive oil in a large skillet over medium heat. Add the potatoes (or other vegetable), onion, and salt. Sauté until vegetables are just cooked through, 5–8 minutes. Remove to a plate to cool slightly.

4 Crack the eggs into a medium bowl. Add the cheese and milk, and whisk to combine. Stir in the spinach leaves and the potato-onion mixture.

5 Using a ladle, divide the egg mixture among the prepared muffin cups.

6 Bake until quiches are firm to the touch, about 25 minutes. Let them stand for 5 minutes before removing from the tin. Serve warm or at room temperature.

"Quiche" comes from the German word *kuchen*, which means cake.

Oscar's
MONSTER MUFFINS
Makes 12 muffins

These bright green muffins are filled with fresh spinach, but kids won't mind at all! With half whole-wheat flour and an added boost of sweetness from banana, these fiber- and potassium-rich muffins make a fun breakfast or after-school snack.

INGREDIENTS
Cooking spray
1 cup all-purpose flour
1 cup whole-wheat flour
¾ cup granulated sugar
2 teaspoons baking powder
1½ teaspoons cinnamon
½ teaspoon baking soda
½ teaspoon salt
¼ cup canola or vegetable oil
¾ cup low-fat milk
6 cups packed baby spinach leaves (washed, dried, and stems removed)
1 large banana, peeled
2 teaspoons vanilla extract

EQUIPMENT
Measuring cups
Measuring spoons
12-cup standard-size muffin tin
Large mixing bowl
Whisk
Blender or food processor
Toothpick
Cooling rack

1 Preheat the oven to 350°F. Coat a 12-cup muffin tin with the cooking spray.

2 Combine both flours, sugar, baking powder, cinnamon, baking soda, and salt in a large bowl, and whisk to combine.

3 Add the oil, milk, and spinach to a food processor or high-powered blender. Blend until very smooth. Add banana and vanilla, and blend again until smooth.

4 Pour the contents of the food processor or blender into the large bowl with the dry ingredients, and fold them until combined. Spoon the batter into the prepared muffin tin, dividing it evenly and filling the cups about three-quarters full.

5 Bake for 18–20 minutes, or until a toothpick inserted in the center of a muffin comes out clean or with just a few moist crumbs.

6 Cool the muffins in the tin for 10 minutes, then turn them out onto a rack and cool completely.

Seriously Yummy Snacks

When the energy gets low, the snacks come out! Store-bought snacks tend to be high in sugar and salt. With the homemade kind, you and your kids get more control over what you eat. Whether kids are munching on veggies and tasty dips made with low-fat dairy or beans, salsa and guacamole alongside whole-grain chips or crackers, or tasty fruit salad packed with flavor, they can get the delicious boost they need to power through the day.

Elmo's
EVERYDAY HUMMUS
Makes about 2 cups

Homemade hummus is a snap to make and much more healthy, delicious, and cost-effective than the store-bought kind. What's more, you can adjust the seasonings to fit your family's tastes.

INGREDIENTS
1 (14.5-ounce) can garbanzo
    beans (chickpeas), drained
½ cup tahini (sesame seed paste)
1 clove garlic, chopped
⅓ cup freshly squeezed lemon juice (from about 2
    lemons)
⅓ cup water
Salt and ground black pepper
Fresh parsley sprigs, for garnish
Pita bread, cut into triangles and lightly toasted,
    and/or raw vegetable crudités, for dipping

EQUIPMENT
Can opener
Strainer
Measuring cups
Knife
Cutting board
Blender or food processor

1   Place the chickpeas, tahini, garlic, lemon juice, and water in a blender or food processor, and blend until the mixture is creamy, stopping occasionally to scrape down the sides. Add salt and pepper to taste. (Add additional water to thin the consistency if desired.)

2   Serve hummus chilled or at room temperature, garnished with fresh parsley sprigs and accompanied by pita bread or vegetables.

SLIMEY'S SUGGESTION!
Add ⅓ cup roasted, peeled red peppers to the recipe above for a delicious orange hummus.

Oscar's
QUICK PICKLES

Makes 1 jar of pickles

Cucumbers as green as Oscar work well here, of course—but don't be afraid to try other vegetables! Peeled, sliced carrots and red onions also work particularly well for pickling.

INGREDIENTS

½ cup unseasoned rice vinegar
1 tablespoon granulated sugar
2 teaspoons salt
1 cup thinly sliced vegetables such
    as carrots, cucumbers,
    beets, or cabbage

EQUIPMENT

Measuring cups
Measuring spoons
Knife
Cutting board
Medium bowl
Whisk
Large clean jar with lid

1 Place the vinegar, sugar, and salt in a medium bowl. Whisk until the sugar and salt dissolve.

2 Add the vegetable of your choice, and with your (clean!) hands, squeeze it lightly in the vinegar mixture.

3 Let it sit out on the counter for at least 15 minutes, then transfer the vegetables and liquid to a clean jar, cover, and refrigerate. (The pickles last for a few days in the refrigerator and will get more pickle-y as they sit!)

SLIMEY'S SUGGESTION!
Try adding fresh sprigs of dill to the jar for a classic dill pickle.

Snuffleupagus's
LOADED-UP POTATO SKINS
Makes 6–8 servings

These potato skins make a tasty appetizer or weekend snack. And the scooped-out insides of the potatoes can be used to make mashed potatoes for dinner!

INGREDIENTS
4 medium russet potatoes, washed and dried
Olive oil
½ pound bacon, diced
½ teaspoon salt
½ teaspoon ground black pepper
1 cup grated low-fat Cheddar cheese
1 cup low-fat sour cream or plain Greek yogurt
1 bunch chives, minced

EQUIPMENT
Measuring cups
Measuring spoons
Knife
Baking sheet
Aluminum foil
Large skillet
Paper towels
Oven mitt
Cutting board
Small spoon

1 Preheat the oven to 400°F. Line a baking sheet with foil.

2 Rub the potatoes lightly with olive oil to coat them. Place the potatoes on the prepared baking sheet, and bake for about an hour, or until a fork pierces them easily. Remove the baking sheet from the oven, and let the potatoes cool for 10–15 minutes.

3 While the potatoes bake, heat the oil in a large skillet over medium-high heat, then cook the bacon until crisp. Drain on paper towels.

4 Put on an oven mitt. Use it to transfer a potato to the cutting board, then use the hand with the oven mitt to steady the potato while you cut it into halves lengthwise. Repeat for the remaining potatoes. Use a small spoon to scrape out most of the potato flesh from each half. (Save the flesh to eat later!) Return the halves to the foil-lined baking sheet. Sprinkle with salt and pepper.

5 Set the oven to broil. Top each half with bacon and cheese, dividing them evenly among all halves. Broil the halves until the cheese is bubbling. Place the skins on a serving plate. Top each half with a spoonful of sour cream or yogurt and sprinkle with chives. Serve warm.

Rosita's
MANGO SALSA

Makes about 3 cups

This sweet and savory salsa is perfect served with tortilla chips and Oscar's Gooey Guacamole (see p. 44), and makes for a colorful addition to Bert & Ernie's Make-Your-Own Burrito Bowls (see p. 96) or family taco night.

INGREDIENTS

2 fresh mangoes, peeled and chopped (about 2 cups)

½ small red onion, chopped (about ¼ cup)

1 red bell pepper, chopped (about ½ cup) (optional)

1 fresh jalapeño pepper, seeded and chopped (about 3 tablespoons) (optional)

2 limes, juiced (about ¼ cup)

1 clove garlic, minced

Salt, to taste

½ bunch cilantro, carefully washed, stems removed, and finely chopped (about 1 tablespoon) (optional)

Tortilla chips, toasted pita triangles, or raw or steamed vegetables, for dipping

EQUIPMENT

Knife

Cutting board

Measuring cups

Measuring spoons

Medium nonreactive (stainless steel, enamel, or glass) mixing bowl

Plastic wrap

1 Stir together all the ingredients in a medium nonreactive bowl. Cover the bowl with plastic wrap and chill for 1–2 hours before serving.

2 Serve with tortilla chips, toasted pita triangles, or raw or steamed vegetables.

SLIMEY'S SUGGESTION!

If you can't find fresh mangoes, try peaches, nectarines, or even pineapple.

Twiddlebug Tip A grown-up will need to prep the chopped fruits and vegetables, but children can squeeze the limes and mix up the salsa all by themselves.

More mangoes are eaten each day around the world than any other fruit.

Oscar's
GOOEY GUACAMOLE

Makes about 2 cups

Fragrant, creamy guacamole is fun to mash and excellent inside tacos and burritos, or served as an appetizer with tortilla chips. If you can't find ripe avocados, let hard ones sit in a paper bag on your counter for a day or two until they are still firm but yield slightly to light pressure.

INGREDIENTS

2 avocados, peeled and pitted
1 large clove garlic, minced
1½ teaspoons freshly squeezed
    lemon juice
Salt and ground black pepper
Cayenne pepper (optional)
1 tablespoon finely chopped onion (optional)
1 small tomato, chopped (optional)
Tortilla chips, toasted pita triangles, or raw or
    steamed vegetables, for serving

EQUIPMENT

Knife
Cutting board
Measuring spoons
Fork
Medium mixing bowl

1   Mash the avocado flesh with a fork in a medium bowl until somewhat smooth—it should still be a bit chunky. Add garlic, lemon juice, salt, black pepper, and (if using) cayenne pepper to taste. Mix in tomato and onion (if using).

2   Serve with tortilla chips, toasted pita triangles, or raw or steamed vegetables.

SLIMEY'S SUGGESTION!

For a change of pace on weekend mornings, make breakfast tacos with scrambled eggs, refried beans, corn or flour tortillas, and guacamole.

Two-Headed Monster's
TWICE-AS-SWEET FRUIT SALAD

Makes about 4 servings

Who doesn't love a delicious fruit salad? The natural sweetness in the light glaze makes this healthy snack feel like even more of a treat.

INGREDIENTS

Fruit Salad

2 cups strawberries, stemmed and chopped

4 kiwis, peeled and chopped

2 mangoes, peeled, seeded, and chopped

Glaze

1 tablespoon honey, or more to taste

1 tablespoon lemon juice, or more to taste

1 teaspoon lemon zest

EQUIPMENT

Vegetable peeler

Cutting board

Knife

Medium bowl

Measuring spoons

Small bowl

Whisk

1 Make the salad: Combine strawberries, kiwis, and mangoes in a medium bowl.

2 Make the glaze: In a small bowl, whisk together the honey, lemon juice, and lemon zest.

3 Pour the glaze over the fruit to serve.

SLIMEY'S SUGGESTION!

For a refreshing twist, substitute lime juice for the lemon juice and lime zest for the lemon zest.

Twiddlebug Tip Use whatever fruit you have on hand. Children can choose which fruits they want in their snack and taste-test the glaze until it's just right.

Two heads are better than one.

So are two flavors!

Elmo's
ALMOND CRACKERS
Makes 6–8 servings

Crispy, crunchy, and gluten-free, these crackers are perfect for dipping in Elmo's Everyday Hummus (see p. 36).

INGREDIENTS
1 egg
½ teaspoon salt
Pinch of ground black pepper
1¾ cups almond flour

EQUIPMENT
Measuring spoons
Measuring cups
Large bowl
Whisk
2 sheets parchment paper
Rolling pin
Baking sheet
Knife
Cooling rack

1   Preheat the oven to 350°F.

2   Place the egg, salt, and pepper in a large bowl, and whisk to combine. Add the almond flour, stirring until the dough comes together. Knead it gently to form a ball.

3   Place the dough ball on one sheet of parchment paper, patting it down to flatten slightly. Top the dough with the second sheet of parchment paper, and roll until the dough is about ⅛ inch thick. Remove the top sheet of parchment paper, and transfer the bottom sheet with the dough onto a baking sheet, then with a knife cut the dough into 1½-inch squares.

4   Bake for 12–15 minutes, until golden brown. (The crackers at the edges of the pan may brown more quickly; if so, remove them from the baking sheet earlier.) Transfer cooked crackers to a cooling rack. Crackers can be stored in an airtight container at room temperature for up to a week.

SLIMEY'S SUGGESTION!
Mix 1 teaspoon each sesame, poppy, and flax seeds into the dough for crunchy, seedy crackers.

Grover's
CRISPY-CRUNCHY GARBANZO BEANS

Makes 4–6 servings

Kids can down these simple, delicious homemade snacks by the handful. And since they're an excellent source of protein, you won't mind at all! In an airtight container, they'll keep for a week in the fridge but will lose their crunch, so they're best eaten soon after they're baked.

INGREDIENTS

2 tablespoons olive oil
1 tablespoon low-sodium soy sauce
1 teaspoon freshly squeezed lemon juice
1 (15-ounce) can garbanzo beans (chickpeas), drained and rinsed
Salt and pepper to taste

EQUIPMENT

Can opener
Strainer
Measuring spoons
Baking sheet
Parchment paper or aluminum foil
Large mixing bowl
Whisk
Paper towels
Cooling rack

1 Preheat the oven to 400°F. Line a baking sheet with parchment paper or aluminum foil.

2 In a large bowl, whisk together the olive oil, soy sauce, and lemon juice.

3 Pat the garbanzo beans dry with paper towels, then add the beans to the olive oil mixture and stir to combine. Spread the beans out on the prepared baking sheet.

4 Bake for 30 minutes, stirring once halfway through. Remove the baking sheet from the oven and cool on a rack. Sprinkle them with salt and pepper, to taste. Serve the beans warm or at room temperature.

SLIMEY'S SUGGESTION!
Sprinkle these on salads in place of croutons.

Big Bird's
RAINBOW ROLLS
Makes 8–10 rolls

A rainbow of vegetables fills these beautiful snack rolls. Kids will love watching the rice paper wrappers transform in the warm water.

INGREDIENTS
3 carrots, peeled and cut into thin strips
1 cucumber, peeled and cut into thin strips
3–4 leaves romaine lettuce, cut into thin strips
1 ripe mango, peeled, pitted, and cut into thin strips
1 (6- or 8-ounce) package baked, seasoned tofu, cut into thin strips
2 bunches fresh herbs (like basil, cilantro, or mint)
8–10 rice paper wrappers (22 centimeters, or about 8½ inches, in diameter)

EQUIPMENT
Vegetable peeler
Knife
Cutting board
Shallow dish
Clean kitchen towel
Platter, for serving
Paper towels

1 When you're ready to assemble the rolls, pour warm water into a shallow dish. Wet a kitchen towel and wring it out. Spread it out next to the water dish. Place the sliced vegetables and mango, tofu, and herbs close by.

2 Slide one rice paper wrapper into the water to soften. Depending on the brand of wrapper, it should take only between 15 and 60 seconds. Once it's floppy, it's ready!

3 Remove the rice paper wrapper from the water and place it on the clean kitchen towel, gently spreading out the wrapper's edges into a circle.

4 Place a few strips each of vegetables, mango, and tofu on the bottom third of the wrapper. Top with a few strips of lettuce and a couple of herb leaves or sprigs. Bring the bottom of the rice sheet up to cover the pile of strips and roll over once. Next, fold in the sides of the circles and fold over the middle. Continue rolling up the rest of the way. The damp rice paper should stick to itself and seal. If things are falling out, you may have put in too many ingredients—but it will still taste good!

5 Put your finished roll on a platter, seam side down. Cover the rolls with damp paper towels while you make the rest. Serve at room temperature or chilled. Rolls keep for a day in an airtight container in the refrigerator.

Zoe's
MELON SOUP
Makes 6–8 servings

Made with a cantaloupe, this soup is Zoe orange, but you can use a green honeydew as well. It's sweet and refreshing, and while you can certainly drink it, it's more fun to eat it with a spoon!

INGREDIENTS
1 (3- to 4-pound) very ripe
    cantaloupe or
    honeydew melon
Zest and juice of 1 lime
1 sprig of mint, leaves picked off, stem
    discarded (plus more mint for garnish if desired)
½ cup plain nonfat Greek yogurt
¼ cup mild olive oil
Pinch of salt

EQUIPMENT
Knife
Cutting board
Measuring spoons
Measuring cups
Blender

1   Peel and seed the melon, then chop it into chunks. Transfer the melon, plus any juices from the cutting board, into a blender.

2   Add the lime zest, 1 tablespoon of the lime juice, the mint leaves, yogurt, oil, and salt to the blender. Blend on high speed until very smooth. Taste and adjust seasonings with more salt or lime juice until it's just how you like it.

3   Cover the blender, and place the whole thing in the refrigerator until the soup is very cold, about an hour. Stir and serve in fun glasses or bowls, garnished with mint.

SLIMEY'S SUGGESTION!
If you put the whole melon in the fridge the day before you start, the soup won't need as much time to chill afterward.

55

Prairie Dawn's
RANCH DIP & VEGGIES
Makes about 1½ cups dip

Homemade ranch dip is so much tastier and healthier than any you can find at the store.

INGREDIENTS
½ cup low-fat mayonnaise
½ cup nonfat plain Greek yogurt
1 clove garlic, minced
1½ teaspoons chopped fresh dill (or 1 teaspoon dried dill)
2 tablespoons chopped fresh parsley
3 tablespoons chopped fresh chives
½ teaspoon freshly squeezed lemon juice
Salt and ground black pepper
Raw vegetables (carrots, peppers, cucumbers, etc.), for serving

EQUIPMENT
Measuring cups
Measuring spoons
Knife
Cutting board
Whisk
Medium bowl

1 In a medium bowl, whisk the first seven ingredients until well combined. Add salt and pepper to taste.

2 Transfer the bowl to the refrigerator and chill at least 30 minutes so that the flavors can meld together.

3 While the dip is chilling, prepare the veggies: Wash the vegetables, peel if desired, and cut into sticks or bite-sized pieces.

4 Serve the veggies alongside a small bowl of the ranch dressing, and let kids get dipping! Any leftover ranch dip can be stored in an airtight container in the refrigerator for up to a week.

SLIMEY'S SUGGESTION!
You can replace the mayonnaise in this dip with an equal amount of Greek yogurt for an even healthier snack.

Sensational Sides

Salads, slaws, and side dishes—sometimes they're the best part of a meal! They give kids a chance to try more flavors, textures, and colors. If kids are mixing dressings, snapping green beans, tossing coleslaw, and peeling carrots, they will be more likely to try adding more fun, colorful, and tasty foods to their plates.

Grover's
RAINBOW RICE SALAD

Makes 4 servings

Filled with colorful veggies and topped with a bright, tangy dressing, this rice salad is as beautiful as it is yummy. It can be served as a side dish or as a main course, and is equally delicious served warm, at room temperature, or chilled, making it great for leftovers.

INGREDIENTS

3 tablespoons olive oil or vegetable oil
1 tablespoon red wine vinegar
1 teaspoon Dijon mustard
Salt and ground black pepper
3 cups cooked brown rice
8 ounces cooked ham, diced (optional)
2 medium tomatoes, chopped
2 ribs celery, finely chopped
2 carrots, finely chopped
1 cucumber, peeled, seeded, and finely chopped
2 scallions, chopped
1 tablespoon finely chopped parsley

EQUIPMENT

Measuring spoons
Measuring cups
Knife
Cutting board
Vegetable peeler
Large serving bowl
Whisk

1   Make the dressing: In a large serving bowl, whisk together the oil, vinegar, and mustard, plus a pinch each of salt and pepper. Add the cooked brown rice, and toss to combine.

2   Add the ham if you're using it, as well as the tomatoes, celery, carrots, cucumber, scallions, and parsley; toss to combine. Season with salt and pepper to taste. Allow the salad to rest a bit so that all the flavors can mingle. Serve warm, at room temperature, or chilled.

SLIMEY'S SUGGESTION!

Rice combines beautifully with a wide variety of foods to make an endless array of tasty salads. Consider using this rice salad as a basic template. You can add other vegetables, fish or meat, nuts, and fruits, as well as eggs, herbs, cheeses, and seeds.

Young kids can help add the chopped vegetables and toss the salad. Older children can help slice softer vegetables like cucumbers and tomatoes (with adult supervision).

Eating your colors is fun! Did you know that carrots can be red, orange, yellow, purple, and white?

Cookie Monster's
MUNCH! CRUNCH! PEANUT SLAW
Makes 4 servings

This slaw is bright green and filled with crunch. For a vegetarian feast, pair it with Count's Chili with Three Beans (see p. 78) and Rosita's Calypso Corn Muffins (see p. 16).

INGREDIENTS
½ cabbage, shredded (about 2 cups)
2 ribs celery, finely chopped (about ½ cup)
3 tablespoons low-fat or nonfat plain yogurt
3 tablespoons mayonnaise
½ teaspoon salt
3 scallions, chopped (about 2 tablespoons)
¼ green pepper, chopped (about 2 tablespoons)
¼ cucumber, peeled and chopped (about ¼ cup)
½ cup lightly salted peanuts, coarsely chopped

EQUIPMENT
Grater
Vegetable peeler
Knife
Cutting board
Measuring cups
Measuring spoons
Large mixing bowl
Medium mixing bowl

1 In a large bowl, toss the cabbage and celery together. Chill for at least an hour.

2 In a separate medium bowl, mix together the yogurt, mayonnaise, salt, scallions, green pepper, and cucumber; chill for at least an hour.

3 Transfer the yogurt mixture into the bowl with the cabbage and celery; toss to combine all ingredients. Sprinkle the chopped peanuts on top, and serve immediately.

SLIMEY'S SUGGESTION!
If anyone in your family has peanut allergies, try this salad with toasted sesame seeds or toasted slivered almonds in place of the peanuts.

Twiddlebug Tip As you're preparing the salad, have kids try the different vegetable ingredients—and the nuts!—to see which one gives them the biggest crunch.

"Coleslaw" comes from the Dutch word *koolsalad*, which means cabbage salad.

Bert & Ernie's
SLIGHTLY NUTTY GREEN BEANS
Makes 6 servings

Fresh green beans are full of flavor, and everyone will love the crunchy, buttery topping on this classic side dish.

INGREDIENTS
2 pounds fresh green beans, ends trimmed
2 tablespoons unsalted butter
1–2 teaspoons salt (or seasoned salt)
½ cup pecan halves or pieces

EQUIPMENT
Measuring spoons
Measuring cups
Medium saucepan
Strainer
Serving bowl
Small saucepan

1 Cut or break the beans into bite-sized pieces. Fill a medium saucepan with water and bring to a boil. Add beans and blanch for about 2 minutes, until they are tender-crisp. Drain and transfer to a serving bowl or platter.

2 In a small saucepan, melt the butter. Add the salt and pecans, and sauté over low heat until the nuts are slightly browned, 2–3 minutes.

3 Pour the butter and nut mixture over the beans. Serve immediately.

SLIMEY'S SUGGESTION!
For a nut-free version, try toasting bread crumbs with the salt and butter instead of pecans.

Snuffy's
PUFFY FOCACCIA BREAD
Makes 6–8 servings

Focaccia bread is similar to a puffy pizza dough—crunchy on the outside, soft and chewy on the inside. It goes perfectly with soups or stews, or, cut in half, it's an excellent alternative to sandwich bread.

INGREDIENTS
4 cups all-purpose flour
1½ teaspoons salt
1 teaspoon instant/rapid-rise yeast
2 cups lukewarm water
3 tablespoons olive oil, divided
Kosher salt for finishing (about ¾ teaspoon)

EQUIPMENT
Measuring cups
Measuring spoons
Large mixing bowl
Whisk
Wooden spoon
Clean kitchen towel or plastic wrap
Large rimmed baking sheet
Fork
Cooling rack

1 In a large bowl, whisk together the flour, salt, and yeast. Add the water and mix with a wooden spoon (or your hands) until combined, forming a sticky dough. Cover the bowl with a clean kitchen towel or plastic wrap and set it in a warm spot to rise for about 1½ hours, until roughly doubled in size.

2 Preheat the oven to 425°F.

3 Pour 2 tablespoons of the olive oil onto a rimmed baking sheet, spreading it around to coat the entire surface. Use a fork to pull the dough from the sides of the bowl, shaping it into a ball—this will deflate it slightly. Place the dough ball onto the prepared baking sheet, and roll it to coat it in the oil.

4 Let the dough rest uncovered for 20 minutes. Drizzle the remaining tablespoon olive oil over the dough, and pull and stretch it to fill the baking sheet, keeping it approximately the same thickness throughout. (If your dough isn't stretching properly, let it rest for an additional 5–10 minutes, then try again.) Press your fingertips lightly into the dough to dimple the entire surface.

5 Sprinkle with the salt and bake for 20–25 minutes, until golden brown. Place the baking sheet on a rack to cool. Serve warm or at room temperature.

Cookie Monster's
MOROCCAN CARROT SALAD

Makes 4–6 servings

This bright, colorful salad is especially welcome in the winter months, but it's also a great side dish for summer barbecues.

INGREDIENTS

Salad

2 pounds carrots, washed and ends trimmed
3 tablespoons chopped parsley
3 tablespoons chopped cilantro

Dressing

¾ teaspoon salt
1 teaspoon ground cumin
½ teaspoon ground cinnamon
Pinch of red pepper flakes or smoked
    paprika (optional)
Juice of 1 lemon (about 2 tablespoons)
¼ cup olive oil
1 tablespoon toasted sesame seeds (optional)

EQUIPMENT

Knife
Cutting board
Measuring spoons
Measuring cups
Box grater, vegetable peeler, or food processor
    with grating attachment
Serving bowl
Small mixing bowl
Whisk

1 Make the salad: Peel and grate the carrots with a box grater or food processor with grating attachment, or use a peeler to create long carrot ribbons. If the grating is too time-consuming, you can slice the carrots thinly. Place them in a serving bowl.

2 Add the chopped herbs and toss to mix.

3 Make the dressing: Place the salt and the spices in a small bowl. Add the lemon juice, and whisk until the salt dissolves. Whisk in the oil.

4 Pour the dressing over the carrots and toss to mix. Sprinkle with sesame seeds, if desired. Serve immediately.

SLIMEY'S SUGGESTION!
Try using different colored carrots to make a rainbow salad.

69

Zoe's
BAKED SWEET POTATO FRIES
Makes 4 servings

Every kid loves french fries. This sweet-savory version, made with nutrient-rich sweet potatoes, is even better than the original, and healthier because it's baked, not fried.

INGREDIENTS
1 pound (about 3 medium-sized) sweet potatoes, peeled and cut into ¼-inch slices
2 tablespoons cornstarch
½ teaspoon salt, plus more for sprinkling
3–4 tablespoons olive oil or vegetable oil

EQUIPMENT
Vegetable peeler
Knife
Cutting board
Measuring spoons
2 rimmed baking sheets
Parchment paper or aluminum foil
Large mixing bowl
Cooling rack

1 Preheat the oven to 425°F. Arrange racks in upper and lower thirds of the oven. Line the baking sheets with parchment paper or aluminum foil.

2 Place the sweet potatoes into a large mixing bowl. Add the cornstarch and salt, and toss until the cornstarch is absorbed. Add the oil, and toss until the potatoes are well covered.

3 Spread the sweet potatoes equally and in an even layer, dividing them between the two baking sheets, making sure not to crowd the sheets.

4 Roast for 20–30 minutes, until the potatoes are crisp on the outside and tender on the inside, tossing the potatoes and rotating the baking sheets midway through baking.

5 Sprinkle with more salt if desired, and transfer to a wire rack to cool slightly. Serve warm.

SLIMEY'S SUGGESTION!
Sweet potato fries are a great snack on their own. But try tossing them with herbs such as rosemary or parsley. They also go well as a side with Rosita's Meatball Sandwiches (see p. 90).

Twiddlebug Tip Ketchup is a natural dipping sauce for sweet potato fries, but what about trying Prairie Dawn's Ranch Dip (see p. 56)? Or ask your kids to create their own dipping sauce!

Sweet potatoes can be white, purple, yellow, or orange!

Grover's
CRUSHED CUCUMBER SALAD

Makes 4 servings

Crushing cucumbers exposes a lot of craggy surface area to soak up this delicious dressing. The salad is best served chilled, so try to make it a couple of hours before you plan to eat it and let it rest in the refrigerator.

INGREDIENTS

2 English cucumbers, washed
¾ teaspoon salt
2 teaspoons granulated sugar
1½ tablespoons unseasoned rice vinegar (or another white vinegar)
2 teaspoons toasted sesame oil
2 teaspoons soy sauce
1 tablespoon vegetable oil
1–2 cloves garlic, minced

EQUIPMENT

Knife
Cutting board
Measuring spoons
Rolling pin
Large serving bowl
Small bowl
Whisk

1   Cut off the ends of the washed cucumbers, then cut each cucumber into four pieces.

2   Using a rolling pin, press down on the sliced cucumber so they crack and break into smaller pieces. (If you don't have a rolling pin, you can also use a knife to cut the cucumbers into smaller chunks.) Place the cucumber pieces in a large serving bowl.

3   Place the salt, sugar, and vinegar in a small bowl, and whisk until the salt and sugar dissolve. Add the sesame oil, soy sauce, vegetable oil, and garlic, and whisk again.

4   Pour the dressing over the cucumbers, and use your hands to toss it together. Refrigerate for 30 minutes to an hour, then serve cold.

SLIMEY'S SUGGESTION!

You can substitute slicing cucumbers for English cucumbers, or if you can find them, try Persian cucumbers. These are smaller cucumbers and can be found in some grocery stores and specialty markets.

Twiddlebug Tip Smashing the cucumbers might take some grown-up assistance, but kids will have fun trying to crush a vegetable they most often see sliced. They can also help by tossing the cucumbers in the dressing with their (clean) hands.

Make sure to put your leftover salad in the fridge so that it stays cool as a cucumber!

Abby's
RAINBOW-TASTIC VEGETABLE HASH
Makes 4 servings

This quick-cooking vegetable dish is a lot like ratatouille, a traditional French stew. It brings color and flavor to just about any meal and goes especially well with simple baked chicken breasts or fish.

INGREDIENTS

3 tablespoons olive oil
1 small onion, finely chopped
1 teaspoon fresh thyme
⅛ teaspoon salt
1 small red bell pepper, seeded and diced
4 large cremini mushrooms, coarsely chopped
2 small zucchinis, ends trimmed, diced
1 small clove garlic, minced

EQUIPMENT

Measuring spoons
Knife
Cutting board
Large skillet with lid

1 In a large skillet, heat the oil over medium-high heat. Add the onion and thyme, and reduce the heat. Cook, stirring occasionally, for about 7 minutes, or until the onion is soft and translucent.

2 Stir in the salt, bell pepper, mushrooms, zucchini, and garlic. Cover and cook, stirring occasionally, 4 minutes longer. Remove from the heat and serve.

SLIMEY'S SUGGESTION!

For a nice breakfast or lunch, turn this into a rainbow veggie scramble by scrambling the vegetables with 3 eggs.

Twiddlebug Tip Mushrooms are softer than most vegetables, so even younger children can tear the mushrooms with their hands.

Mushrooms aren't actually vegetables—they're fungi!

75

Mmm, Main Dishes

No matter how busy the day, when you can come together to eat a meal as a family, everyone wins. Sharing stories and enjoying food with grown-ups helps kids' brains and bodies grow. They are seeing the adults they love model healthy eating habits, and they are learning important social skills through your mealtime conversations. And when kids help make the main course, they get to feel the joy of sharing nourishing food with the people they love.

Count's
CHILI WITH THREE BEANS
Makes 8 servings

Loaded with veggies, protein, and warming spices, this healthy vegetarian chili is the perfect family meal. Try it with Snuffy's Puffy Focaccia Bread (see p. 66).

INGREDIENTS

3 tablespoons vegetable or olive oil

2 large yellow onions, coarsely chopped (about 4 cups)

1–2 tablespoons chili powder, or to taste

1 tablespoon ground cumin

1 tablespoon dried oregano

1 teaspoon cayenne pepper (optional)

¼ teaspoon ground cinnamon

1 (28-ounce) can Italian plum tomatoes

3 cups low-sodium chicken broth

2 large bell peppers (any color), stemmed, cored, and cut into ½-inch dice

1½ cups fresh or frozen green beans

1 zucchini, stemmed and chopped

2 ears fresh corn, off the cob, or 1½ cups frozen corn kernels

1 (19-ounce) can dark red kidney beans, rinsed and drained

1 (19-ounce) can pinto beans, rinsed and drained

Salt and ground black pepper

Garnishes of your choice (such as chopped carrots or scallions, low-fat sour cream, or shredded Cheddar cheese)

EQUIPMENT

Measuring cups

Knife

Cutting board

Measuring spoons

Can opener

Strainer

Heavy 5-quart pot or dutch oven with lid

Small bowls, for toppings

1 In a heavy 5-quart pot or dutch oven, warm the oil over medium heat. Add the onions, lower the heat slightly, and cook, stirring, for 8 minutes, or until onions are translucent and tender. Stir in the chili powder, cumin, oregano, cayenne pepper, and cinnamon, and cook, stirring constantly, for 5 minutes.

2 Add the tomatoes with their juice, and chicken broth or water. Bring to a boil, then lower the heat to a simmer and cook, partially covered, for 25 minutes, stirring occasionally.

3 Stir in the bell peppers, and cook for 20 minutes more.

4 Stir in the green beans, zucchini, corn, kidney beans, and pinto beans. Add salt and pepper to taste, and cook for another 15 minutes.

5 Remove from heat. Allow the chili to rest for an hour or two before serving. Reheat and serve warm, with garnishes in small bowls on the side.

Me-Love-Veggies
MAC & CHEESE
Makes 8 servings

You don't have to look too hard to find a kid who loves mac and cheese. This variation on the classic dish has less fat than the traditional version and introduces colorful vegetables.

INGREDIENTS
Cooking spray, for greasing
½ cup dried bread crumbs (optional)
2 cups shredded reduced-fat Cheddar cheese, divided
8 ounces (½ pound) whole-wheat pasta, such as rotelle, macaroni, or bowties
2 heads broccoli, cut into bite-sized pieces (about 4 cups)
1 (14½-ounce) can diced tomatoes
3 tablespoons unsalted butter
3 tablespoons all-purpose flour
2 cups nonfat milk, heated
1 cup shredded Gouda cheese
Salt and ground black pepper

EQUIPMENT
Measuring cups
Measuring spoons
Knife
Cutting board
Can opener
13 x 9-inch (3-quart) shallow baking dish
Large pot
Small mixing bowl
Medium saucepan
Whisk

1 Preheat the oven to 375°F. Coat the 3-quart shallow baking dish with the cooking spray.

2 In a small bowl, stir together the bread crumbs, if using, and ½ cup of the Cheddar cheese.

3 Cook the pasta in a large pot according to package directions. When there are 3 minutes left in the cooking time, stir in the broccoli. Cook 2–3 minutes, until the pasta is tender but firm, and the broccoli is bright green and tender-crisp. Drain well, then immediately return pasta and broccoli to the large pot. Stir in the tomatoes with their juice.

4 While the pasta cooks, melt the butter in a medium saucepan, then slowly add the flour, whisking constantly until a paste forms, about 2 minutes. Slowly add the milk, stirring constantly. Bring to a boil, whisking frequently, until the sauce thickens. Turn the heat to low, and cook 2 minutes longer, whisking constantly until the mixture is smooth. Remove the pan from the heat, and immediately stir in the Gouda and the remaining Cheddar, until the cheeses melt and the sauce is smooth, about 1 minute.

5 Add the sauce to the pasta and vegetables, and mix. Add salt and pepper to taste.

6 Transfer the mixture to the prepared baking dish. Sprinkle the bread crumb–cheese mixture evenly over the top. Bake until the top is light brown and the sauce is bubbling, about 20 minutes.

Twiddlebug Tip Sprinkling the bread crumb–cheese mixture over the top of the mac and cheese before it goes in the oven is the perfect job for kids of all ages.

Next time you smile for the camera, try saying "macaroni" instead of "cheese"!

Ernie's
FAVORITE TUNA NOODLE CASSEROLE

Makes 4 servings

Tuna noodle casserole is a classic for a reason. It's filled with comforting flavors, plus you can keep almost all the ingredients on hand, so it's easy to make anytime.

INGREDIENTS

Cooking spray, for greasing
1 (10.75-ounce) can reduced-sodium cream of
    mushroom soup
½ cup low-fat sour cream
8 ounces egg noodles, cooked according to
    package instructions and drained
½ cup frozen green peas
¼ cup sliced Baby Bella mushrooms
2 (6-ounce) cans tuna, packed in
    water, drained and flaked
Milk
2 tablespoons bread crumbs (optional)

EQUIPMENT

Large pot
Can opener
Measuring cups
Measuring spoons
Strainer
1½-quart casserole dish

1   Preheat the oven to 400°F. Coat a 1½-quart casserole dish with the cooking spray.

2   Pour the soup and sour cream into the casserole dish. Stir in the noodles, peas, mushrooms, and tuna. Add a little milk if the mixture is not moist enough to suit your taste.

3   Bake, uncovered, for about 20 minutes. Stir thoroughly.

4   Scatter the bread crumbs, if using, evenly over the tuna mixture, then bake 5 minutes more, until they are lightly browned and the mixture is bubbling. Serve hot.

SLIMEY'S SUGGESTION!

Turn this classic dish into a "tuna melt" by adding ½ cup shredded Cheddar or Swiss cheese to the bread crumbs before topping and baking.

Oscar's
IT'S-SO-EASY-BEING-GREEN PIZZA
Makes 4 servings

As green as the Grouch himself, this tasty dish is really one part pizza, one part salad. Kids are more likely to get excited about a pile of crisp, tasty greens if they are helping add them to this fun and unique dish.

INGREDIENTS

Cooking spray, for greasing

1 (10-ounce) prebaked whole-wheat or multigrain pizza crust

1–2 cups red tomato sauce or pesto, as needed

4 small green tomatoes, thinly sliced

2 medium zucchinis, trimmed and chopped

2 scallions, trimmed, cut into rings (both white and green parts)

½ cup shredded part-skim mozzarella cheese

1 tablespoon olive oil or vegetable oil

1 teaspoon balsamic vinegar

1 clove garlic, peeled

½ teaspoon dried (or 1 teaspoon fresh minced) oregano, marjoram, or basil (or a combination)

¼ teaspoon salt

Ground black pepper (optional)

3 cups lettuce or greens of your choice, such as arugula, spinach, romaine, or Boston

2 tablespoons grated Parmesan cheese

EQUIPMENT

Knife

Cutting board

Measuring cups

Measuring spoons

Baking sheet

Large bowl

Whisk

1 Preheat the oven to 450°F. Coat the baking sheet with the cooking spray, and place the pizza crust on the baking sheet.

2 Spread the sauce over the crust, to the edges.

3 Arrange the sliced tomatoes, zucchini, and scallions on the pizza crust. Sprinkle the mozzarella evenly over the vegetables. Bake until the vegetables are softened and the mozzarella is melted and bubbly, 10–15 minutes.

4 While the pizza bakes, in a large bowl, combine the oil, vinegar, garlic, herbs, and salt. Whisk vigorously to blend; discard the garlic and add pepper to taste. Add the greens; toss gently.

5 Slide the baked pizza onto a large cutting board. Top the pizza with the greens. Sprinkle with the Parmesan. Cut into slices and serve warm.

Elmo's
RED LENTIL SOUP
Makes 8 servings

Red lentils—which actually turn yellow when cooked—are packed with iron and protein and have a rich, nutty taste that goes great with veggies and pasta in a soup. This dish is easy to pull together and makes for a wonderful weeknight supper all by itself!

INGREDIENTS
2 tablespoons olive oil
1 medium yellow onion, chopped
2 carrots, peeled and chopped
2 celery ribs, chopped
2 cloves garlic, minced
1 teaspoon salt
½ teaspoon ground black pepper
1 (14.5-ounce) can diced tomatoes
1 pound (2⅓ cups) dried red lentils, rinsed and picked over
9 cups water or broth
4–6 fresh thyme sprigs

2 cups dried elbow pasta
8 ounces (1½ cups) fresh spinach, washed and trimmed (or one 10-ounce package frozen spinach, thawed and drained)
Grated Parmesan cheese, for garnish
8 sprigs parsley, for garnish (optional)

EQUIPMENT
Vegetable peeler
Measuring spoons
Knife
Cutting board
Measuring cups
Can opener
Large heavy pot with lid

1 Heat the oil in a large heavy pot over medium heat. Add the onion, carrots, celery, garlic, salt, and pepper, and sauté until all the vegetables are tender, 5–8 minutes. Add the tomatoes with their juices; reduce the heat and simmer until the juices evaporate a little and the tomatoes break down, stirring occasionally, about 8 minutes.

2 Add the lentils and mix to coat. Add the water or broth and stir. Add the thyme sprigs. Bring to a boil over high heat. Cover, reduce the heat to a simmer, and cook until the lentils are almost tender, about 30 minutes.

3 Stir in the pasta. Simmer until the pasta is tender but still firm to the bite, about 8 minutes. Stir in the spinach. Taste and adjust seasoning.

4 Divide the soup among eight bowls. Sprinkle with the Parmesan cheese, garnish with parsley, and serve.

Kids can help measure the correct amount of pasta and sprinkle Parmesan cheese over the bowls at the table for serving.

People have been eating lentils since ancient times. They've even been found in Egyptian tombs!

Grover's
WORLD-TRAVELER RAMEN
Makes 4 servings

Ramen noodles, usually prepared in soup, are extremely popular in Japan, but they originally came from China. This basic recipe is simple and nutritious, and is a great opportunity for kids to experiment by trying some veggies that might be unfamiliar to them.

INGREDIENTS
1 pound boneless, skinless chicken pieces
4–5 cups water or chicken broth
1 medium yellow onion, finely chopped
1 carrot, peeled and chopped
1 celery rib, chopped
2 scallions, trimmed and sliced into rings
2 baby bok choy, washed, trimmed, and chopped
1 cup frozen, shelled edamame
1 (3-ounce) package enoki (straw) mushrooms,
    fresh or frozen
2 (3-ounce) packets ramen noodles,
    seasoning packet discarded

Dash of low-sodium soy sauce
Dash of toasted sesame oil

EQUIPMENT
Measuring cups
Knife
Cutting board
Vegetable peeler
Can opener
Strainer
Large saucepan

1 Place the chicken in a large saucepan, cover with 4–5 cups of water or broth, and bring to a boil. Add the onion, carrot, and celery. Reduce the heat to a simmer, and cook for 30–40 minutes, or until the chicken is cooked through.

2 Remove the chicken from the pot, allow to cool slightly, then cut into bite-sized pieces. Strain and reserve the broth. Discard the vegetables, and return the broth to the saucepan. If necessary, add enough water to create a full 4 cups. Place the chicken pieces back in the broth.

3 Add the scallions, baby bok choy, edamame, and enoki (straw) mushrooms to the broth. Bring to a boil, then reduce the heat to a simmer and cook for 5–7 minutes.

4 Add the ramen noodles, and stir to break them up. Cook for about 3 minutes, or until noodles are soft. Add a dash each of soy sauce and sesame oil, stirring to combine. Divide the soup among four bowls and serve hot.

Twiddlebug Tip Ask kids to choose one or two additional veggies to add to the soup. Every vegetable gives the soup a fun and unique taste, so this recipe offers a lot of room for young chefs to experiment.

In lots of countries, people eat soup for breakfast, too!

Rosita's
MEATBALL SANDWICHES
Makes 4 servings

Everybody knows spaghetti and meatballs. But putting meatballs, marinara sauce, and melty provolone cheese on crispy bread is a different comfort food altogether.

INGREDIENTS

Meatballs

Olive oil, for greasing and brushing
1 pound ground turkey or chicken
½ cup bread crumbs
¼ cup finely grated Parmesan cheese
1 egg
1 clove garlic, minced
1 small yellow onion, finely diced

1 tablespoon minced fresh parsley
½ teaspoon dried oregano

Sandwiches

4 hero or French sandwich rolls, split lengthwise
Baked meatballs, from above
1½ cups jarred marinara sauce, heated
8 slices provolone cheese

EQUIPMENT

Medium saucepan
Pastry or silicone brush
Measuring cups
Knife
Cutting board
Measuring spoons
2 baking sheets
Aluminum foil
Large mixing bowl
Fork
Plastic wrap
Cooling rack

1 Preheat the oven to 400°F. Line a baking sheet with aluminum foil and lightly brush with olive oil.

2 Place the ground meat, bread crumbs, and Parmesan in a large bowl and mix with a fork to combine. Add the egg, garlic, onion, and herbs, and mix gently to combine. Cover the bowl with plastic wrap and refrigerate for 15–30 minutes.

3 Shape the mixture into balls 1½ inches in diameter. Place the balls on the foil-lined baking sheet. Brush the tops of the meatballs with olive oil and bake for 20–25 minutes, or until lightly browned and cooked through. Set the baking sheet on a rack to cool.

4 Position an oven rack in the top third of the oven. Place the rolls, cut sides up, on the second baking sheet. Top the bottom half of each of the four rolls with three or four meatballs, a large dollop of marinara sauce, and two slices of provolone cheese. Broil, checking frequently (you might need to remove sandwich tops earlier), until the cheese is melted, about 2 minutes. Close up sandwiches and serve warm.

Twiddlebug Tip Kids can help assemble the sandwiches prior to broiling. They decide how many meatballs they want on their sandwich and count them out.

Can you think of other foods that are round?

Cookie Monster's
EXTRA-SUPER-GREEN PESTO PASTA
Makes 4–6 servings

This tasty pesto gets an added boost of green from spinach leaves and pumpkin seeds.

INGREDIENTS
4 cups loosely packed basil leaves, washed and dried
1 cup loosely packed spinach leaves, washed and dried
2 tablespoons raw, hulled pumpkin seeds
½ teaspoon salt
¾ cup olive oil
1 small clove garlic, peeled
⅓ cup finely grated Parmesan cheese
1 pound dried farfalle pasta (or any shape of your choosing)

EQUIPMENT
Measuring cups
Measuring spoons
Food processor or blender
Large pot
Strainer
Large serving bowl

1 Place the first six ingredients in the bowl of a food processor or blender. Process until smooth. Add more olive oil if the mixture appears too dry.

2 Add the Parmesan cheese and pulse to combine. The pesto should have the consistency of a thick, wet paste now. Taste and adjust seasonings. Set aside.

3 Cook the pasta according to package instructions. Drain, then transfer to a large serving bowl. Top with 1 cup pesto and toss to coat, adding additional pesto if desired. Serve warm or at room temperature. Any leftover pesto can be frozen in ice-cube trays or will keep for 3–4 days in an airtight container in the refrigerator.

SLIMEY'S SUGGESTION!
Make your pesto pasta extra fancy by adding sliced grilled chicken, halved cherry tomatoes, Kalamata olives, and crumbled feta cheese.

Telly Monster's
NO-FRY FRIED CHICKEN
Makes 4–6 servings

Crispy fried chicken without any of the fuss! Plus it's much healthier to bake it in the oven than it is to fry it in oil.

INGREDIENTS
4 cups seasoned bread crumbs
1 cup Italian salad dressing
1 whole chicken, cut into
    8 pieces, or any combination
    of bone-in thighs, breasts,
    and legs (about 2½ pounds)

EQUIPMENT
Knife
Cutting board
Measuring cups
2 shallow dishes or bowls
Rimmed baking sheet
Aluminum foil

1 Preheat the oven to 350°F. Line a baking sheet with aluminum foil.

2 Pour the bread crumbs into one shallow dish and the salad dressing into another.

3 Dip each piece of chicken first in the dressing, turning to coat, then into the bread crumbs, making sure each piece is completely covered. Place each piece of breaded chicken on the foil-lined baking sheet.

4 Place the baking sheet in the oven and bake for 40–45 minutes until juices run clear when pierced with a knife, or the internal temperature reaches at least 165°F. Serve warm.

SLIMEY'S SUGGESTION!
Along with the bread crumbs, try adding some crushed-up corn-flakes for an extra crunch.

Bert & Ernie's
MAKE-YOUR-OWN BURRITO BOWLS
Makes 4–6 servings

Colorful, healthy, hearty, and endlessly customizable, burrito bowls might become a new family favorite.

INGREDIENTS

1 tablespoon plus 1 teaspoon olive oil
1 clove garlic, minced
1 pound lean ground beef or turkey
½ teaspoon ground cumin
½ teaspoon chili powder
½ teaspoon salt
1 (14.5-ounce) can black beans, rinsed and drained
3 cups cooked brown rice
4–5 leaves romaine lettuce, coarsely chopped
2–3 medium tomatoes, chopped
2 cups low-fat shredded Cheddar or jack cheese
Garnishes of your choice (diced red onion,
    chopped cilantro, low-fat sour cream or nonfat
    plain yogurt, Oscar's Gooey Guacamole from
    p. 44, Rosita's Mango Salsa from p. 42, or
    another salsa)

EQUIPMENT

Measuring spoons
Can opener
Strainer
Measuring cups
Knife
Cutting board
Large skillet
Small saucepan
Small bowls, for toppings

1   In a large skillet, heat 1 tablespoon of the oil over medium-high heat. Add the minced garlic, cooking for 30 seconds or until fragrant. Add the ground meat, cumin, chili powder, and salt, and sauté, stirring, until meat is nicely browned and cooked through, 5–7 minutes. Remove from the heat and set aside.

2   In a small saucepan, heat the beans with the remaining 1 teaspoon of olive oil until warmed through. Set aside.

3   Warm precooked rice in the microwave for 1–2 minutes.

4   Let everyone build their own burrito bowl, topping a scoop of rice with meat, beans, lettuce, tomatoes, cheese, and other garnishes.

Twiddlebug Tip Kids will love preparing the toppings and building their own meal. Place toppings and garnishes in bowls with spoons, and let kids make their own choices.

I like mine with salsa.

I like mine with guacamole!

Rosita's
MOLLETES

Makes 4 servings

One part grilled cheese, one part quesadilla, and all parts delicious.

INGREDIENTS
4 sandwich rolls, halved
4 tablespoons unsalted
    butter, softened
2 cups refried beans, warmed
1½ cups shredded cheese of your choice
Nonfat sour cream, for serving (optional)
Salsa, for serving (optional)

EQUIPMENT
Knife
Cutting board
Measuring cups
Baking sheet

1 Preheat the oven to 400°F.

2 Place the halved rolls cut side up on a baking sheet. Spread a thin layer of butter on the cut side of each roll, dividing the butter evenly among all the rolls. Transfer the baking sheet to the oven, and cook for 5–10 minutes, until the rolls are hot and the tops are just starting to get a little color.

3 Remove the baking sheet from the oven. Spread each roll half with a generous layer of beans, and then sprinkle with cheese.

4 Return the rolls to the oven until the cheese melts and starts to bubble, 8–10 minutes.

5 Divide rolls between four plates, and serve with sour cream and salsa for topping (if using).

SLIMEY'S SUGGESTION!
Serve with Rosita's Mango Salsa (see p. 42) or Oscar's Gooey Guacamole (see p. 44).

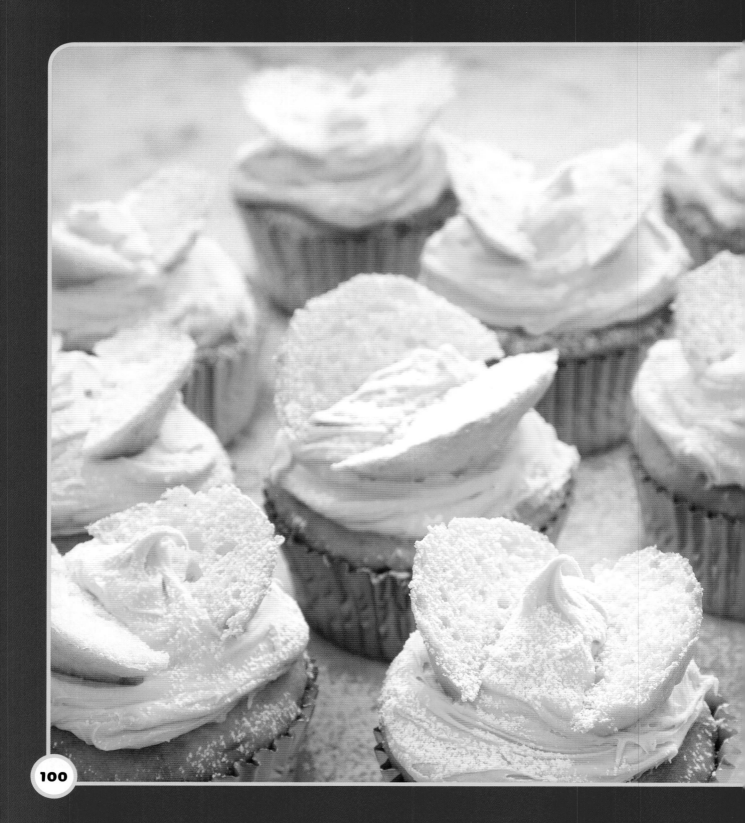

Terrific Treats

Cookie Monster isn't the only one who enjoys a good treat now and then. But as fun as it is to eat dessert, it's even more fun to make it. Stirring doughs, blending frozen treats, slicing juicy fruit, spreading melted chocolate, smelling baking cookies—kids love it all. From crunchy cookies to fruity crisps, these desserts are sure to delight the whole family.

Cookie Monster's
EVERYTHING COOKIE

Makes 2 dozen cookies

This monster of a cookie is fit for a Cookie Monster! It's filled with tons of flavors and textures. Kids will love the novelty of adding cereal to their treats.

INGREDIENTS

Cooking spray, for greasing
½ cup all-purpose flour
¼ cup whole-wheat flour
½ teaspoon baking soda
½ teaspoon salt
1 teaspoon cinnamon
⅛ teaspoon nutmeg
⅛ teaspoon cloves
¾ cup unsalted butter or margarine (12 tablespoons), softened
1 cup firmly packed light-brown sugar
1 egg
1 tablespoon low-fat milk
1 teaspoon vanilla extract
1 cup cornflakes or crisp rice cereal
2 cups old-fashioned rolled oats
½ cup unsweetened shredded coconut
1 cup semisweet chocolate chips
½ cup raisins or dried cranberries

EQUIPMENT

Measuring cups
Measuring spoons
2 baking sheets
Sifter
Medium mixing bowl
Large mixing bowl
Electric mixer
Wooden spoon

1 Preheat the oven to 350°F. Coat the two baking sheets with the cooking spray.

2 In a medium mixing bowl, sift together the flours, baking soda, salt, and spices. Set aside.

3 In a large mixing bowl, cream together the butter and sugar with an electric mixer until light and fluffy. Beat in the egg, then slowly beat in the milk and vanilla. Using a wooden spoon, gradually mix in the sifted ingredients until well blended. Stir in the cereal, oats, coconut, chocolate chips, and dried fruit.

4 Roll the dough into quarter cup–sized balls. Place the balls at least 2 inches apart on the prepared baking sheets and flatten slightly with the palm of your hand. (You may need to bake the cookies in two batches.)

5 Bake for 10–12 minutes, until light golden brown. Allow the cookies to cool on the baking sheets for a few minutes before transferring them to a wire rack to cool completely. Repeat with the remaining dough as needed.

Telly Monster's
ANY-BERRY CRISP
Makes about 8 servings

Pick a berry, any berry! You can make this crisp with fresh-picked or frozen berries, bringing the taste of summer to any season. And if you use frozen, there's no need to thaw the berries before you start baking!

INGREDIENTS
Cooking spray, for greasing
6 cups fresh or frozen berries, such as blueberry, raspberry, or strawberry
1 teaspoon fresh-squeezed lemon juice
3 tablespoons and ½ cup all-purpose flour
⅓ cup granulated sugar or more, depending on the sweetness of the berries

⅔ cup old-fashioned rolled oats
⅓ cup chopped pecans (optional)
⅓ cup packed light-brown sugar
½ teaspoon cinnamon
Pinch of salt
6 tablespoons cold unsalted butter, cut into ½-inch cubes
Vanilla ice cream or frozen yogurt, for serving (optional)

EQUIPMENT
Knife
Cutting board
8 x 8-inch (2-quart) baking dish
Baking sheet
Aluminum foil
Measuring cups
Measuring spoons
2 large mixing bowls
Pastry cutter (optional)
Cooling rack

1 Preheat the oven to 375°F. Lightly grease the baking dish with the cooking spray and line the baking sheet with aluminum foil.

2 In a large mixing bowl, combine berries with lemon juice, 3 tablespoons of the flour, and granulated sugar, using more or less as needed depending on the sweetness of the berries. (Using frozen berries, you will likely need the full ½ cup.) Pour the berry mixture into the prepared baking dish and set aside.

3 In another large mixing bowl, combine the oats, nuts (if using), remaining ½ cup flour, brown sugar, cinnamon, and salt. Add the butter and use a pastry cutter or your fingers to blend it into the dry ingredients. The mixture should appear evenly coarse and crumbly.

4 Cover the berries evenly with the topping, then place the baking dish on the lined baking sheet (in case it bubbles over). Bake for 35–40 minutes, or until the topping is golden. Let cool on a rack for at least 30 minutes. Serve warm or at room temperature, plain or topped with vanilla ice cream or frozen yogurt.

Twiddlebug Tip

Ask kids to think about fruit combinations they might like to try in a crisp like this. Let them invent a recipe with 6 cups of fruit of their choosing, and see what happens!

It tastes like I'm eating a pie and a cookie all at once!

105

Elmo's
SUGAR & SPICE COOKIES
Makes 4–5 dozen cookies

Filled with everything nice, these cookies will make your house smell divine while they're baking. Rolling the cookies in sugar before baking them is a fun task for kids of all ages and results in a beautifully crackly cookie with a little bit of sparkle.

INGREDIENTS
Cooking spray, for greasing
2 cups all-purpose flour
2 teaspoons baking soda
¼ teaspoon salt
1 teaspoon cinnamon
¾ teaspoon cloves
¾ teaspoon ginger
¾ cup shortening or unsalted butter
1 cup granulated sugar, plus more
    for rolling cookies
1 egg
¼ cup molasses

EQUIPMENT
Measuring cups
Measuring spoons
Baking sheet
2 large mixing bowls
Electric mixer
Small bowl

1   Preheat the oven to 375°F. Grease a baking sheet.

2   In a large bowl, mix together the flour, baking soda, salt, and spices, and set aside.

3   In another large bowl, using an electric mixer, cream the shortening with 1 cup sugar and egg until pale and creamy. Add the molasses, and mix thoroughly. Add the dry ingredients, and mix until the dough is moist and well combined.

4   Place the additional granulated sugar in a small bowl. Form the dough into 1-inch balls, then roll them in the granulated sugar. Place the balls about 2 inches apart on the greased baking sheet. Bake for 10–12 minutes.

Abby Cadabby's
PINK FAIRY CAKES

Makes 2 dozen mini cakes

These little cakes look like a group of festive fairies on the serving plate. They're great for celebrations, or any time you want a whimsical treat.

INGREDIENTS

Cakes

Cooking spray, for greasing
1 cup margarine
1 cup superfine sugar
1½ cups all-purpose flour
1 teaspoon baking powder
¼ teaspoon salt
¼ cup low-fat milk
4 eggs
Confectioners' sugar, for
   serving

Frosting

¾ cup (1½ sticks) margarine
1 cup confectioners' sugar
1 teaspoon vanilla
Red food coloring

EQUIPMENT

Measuring cups
Measuring spoons
2 (12-cup) standard-size muffin
   tins
Large mixing bowl

Electric mixer
Wooden spoon
Medium mixing bowl
Small mixing bowl
Whisk
Cooling rack
Knife
Cutting board

1   Preheat the oven to 375°F. Grease two 12-cup muffin tins with the cooking spray.

2   In a large bowl, cream the margarine and sugar together with an electric mixer. In a medium bowl, combine the flour, baking powder, and salt. In a small bowl, whisk together the milk and eggs. Stir in half of the flour mixture to the creamed margarine and superfine sugar. Next, stir in half the milk-egg mixture. Repeat, mixing constantly, until all the ingredients are combined.

3   Pour the batter into the muffin tins and bake for about 15 minutes, until tops are golden. Let cupcakes cool on a cooling rack, then remove from tins.

4   As the cupcakes cool, make the frosting: With an electric mixer, cream together the margarine, 1 cup confectioners' sugar, and vanilla until the mixture reaches the desired consistency. Add a drop or two of food coloring and stir for "Abby pink" frosting.

5   When the cupcakes have cooled, slice off the top part of each one, creating a small round of cake. Spoon a large dollop of frosting over the remaining cupcake. Cut the round slices of the cake in half lengthwise and stick them in the frosting to form the fairy wings. To finish, sift or shake a little confectioners' sugar over the tops of the cakes.

With lots of ingredients to mix together—and then combine—there are plenty of jobs for kids to try.

Tastes fairy-tastic!

Two-Headed Monster's
DOUBLE CHOCOLATE COOKIES

Makes 18 large cookies

What's better than a chocolate cookie? One that's covered in even more chocolate!

INGREDIENTS

Cookies

Cooking spray, for greasing
2 cups all-purpose flour
1 teaspoon baking soda
¼ teaspoon salt
½ cup (1 stick) butter
3 ounces unsweetened
    chocolate
1 cup firmly packed dark-brown
    sugar

1 egg
1 teaspoon vanilla extract
½ cup heavy cream

Glaze

1 ounce unsweetened
    chocolate
1 tablespoon unsalted butter
1½ tablespoons hot water
2 tablespoons heavy cream
1 cup confectioners' sugar

EQUIPMENT

Measuring cups
Measuring spoons
2 baking sheets
Medium mixing bowl
Sifter
Knife
Cutting board
Heavy 3-quart saucepan
Heavy wooden spoon
Cooling rack
Double boiler with lid

1 Preheat the oven to 375°F. Grease the two baking sheets with the cooking spray.

2 In a medium bowl, sift together the flour, baking soda, and salt, and set aside. Cut the butter into ½-inch chunks and place in a heavy 3-quart saucepan. Add the chocolate and cook over low heat, stirring, until melted. Remove from the heat and stir in the sugar with a heavy wooden spoon. Add the egg and the vanilla, and stir until smooth. Stir in half the sifted dry ingredients, and slowly stir in the cream. Add the remaining dry ingredients and stir briskly until the dough is completely smooth.

3 Drop heaping tablespoons of the dough onto the baking sheets, spacing them about 3 inches apart. Bake for 12–15 minutes, or until the cookies appear a bit spongy but firm. Let them rest for a few minutes on the baking sheets, then transfer them to a cooling rack.

4 While the cookies cool, prepare the glaze: In a covered double boiler, or in a microwave-safe bowl in 30-second intervals, melt the chocolate with the butter. Remove the lid and stir in the hot water and the heavy cream. Add the confectioners' sugar and stir until smooth. If necessary, adjust with more water or sugar to make the consistency like a heavy cream sauce. Spoon and smooth the glaze over the tops of the cookies, allowing a ½-inch edge. Allow the glaze to set for about an hour.

Twiddlebug Tip
Kids can help drop spoonfuls of the dough on the baking sheets, and they'll love spreading the glaze over the tops of the cookies.

The Two-Headed Monster likes chocolate inside cookies!

The Two-Headed Monster likes chocolate on top of cookies!

Zoe's
YUMMY CARROT COOKIES
Makes 32 cookies

Almost like mini carrot cakes, this twist on oatmeal raisin cookies is full of hearty, healthy ingredients yet tastes like a treat. They're great for after-school snacks or a special family teatime.

INGREDIENTS
1 cup all-purpose flour
1 teaspoon baking powder
1 teaspoon baking soda
¼ teaspoon salt
½ cup (1 stick) butter
½ cup firmly packed light-brown sugar
1 egg
¾ cup firmly packed grated raw carrots (from about 2 medium carrots)
½ cup old-fashioned rolled oats
½ cup raisins
¾ cup walnuts, coarsely chopped

EQUIPMENT
Measuring cups
Measuring spoons
Grater
2 baking sheets
Aluminum foil
Medium mixing bowl
Sifter
Stand mixer (or large mixing bowl and electric mixer)
Cooling rack

1 Preheat the oven to 350°F. Line two baking sheets with aluminum foil.

2 In a medium bowl, sift together the flour, baking powder, baking soda, and salt, and set aside.

3 Place the butter and sugar in the bowl of a stand mixer, and cream together on medium-high speed (or use an electric mixer and a large bowl). Add the egg and beat to mix. Beat in the grated carrots. Turn the mixer down to low speed, and slowly add the sifted dry ingredients and then the oats, scraping the bowl and beating only until thoroughly mixed. Stir in the raisins and the walnuts.

4 Drop rounded teaspoonfuls of the dough onto the prepared baking sheets, spacing them about 2 inches apart. Bake for about 15 minutes, or until cookies are golden brown. Let them cool on a rack before serving.

Big Bird's
CHOCOLATE YUM-YUM
Makes 40 pieces

In 20 minutes, you could have a pan of these special treats cooling on the counter. When topped with crushed candy canes, this makes a wonderful holiday dessert.

INGREDIENTS
4 ounces soda or saltine crackers (about 40 pieces)
1 cup (2 sticks) unsalted butter
1 cup firmly packed light-brown sugar
2 cups semisweet chocolate chips
¾ cup toppings of your choice, such
    as chopped pecans, chopped
    almonds, or crushed candy canes

EQUIPMENT
Measuring cups
Rimmed baking sheet
Aluminum foil
Small saucepan
Heatproof spatula
Cooling rack

1 Preheat the oven to 400°F. Line a rimmed baking sheet with the aluminum foil.

2 Place the saltine crackers on the baking sheet in a single layer, salt side up. Set aside.

3 Place the butter and sugar in a small saucepan. Cook over medium-high heat, stirring to combine. Bring to a boil, and then boil for 3 minutes without stirring. Turn off the heat, and immediately pour the mixture over the saltines, spreading it with a spatula to cover them.

4 Transfer the baking sheet to the oven and bake for 5 minutes. Remove the sheet from the oven, place it on a cooling rack, and sprinkle the chocolate chips all over the crackers. Let them sit until the chocolate is mostly melted, about 5 minutes. Use a spatula to spread the melted chocolate to cover the crackers, then sprinkle on the toppings of your choice.

5 Let them cool completely, then break the crackers into pieces and serve.

SLIMEY'S SUGGESTION!
For salty chocolate caramel yum-yum, sprinkle on about
½ teaspoon of coarse sea salt instead of the other toppings.

Twiddlebug Tip Kids will love thinking of other toppings for these tasty treats, from nuts and dried fruits to special bite-sized candies.

When should you take a cookie to the doctor? *When it feels crumby!*

Julia's
BANANA–CHOCOLATE CHIP SOFT SERVE

Makes 4 servings

If you freeze bananas and give them a whirl in the food processor, they turn into gooey, thick ice cream—but without the cream or sugar! Adding chocolate chips makes this an extra-special treat.

INGREDIENTS
3 ripe bananas (yellow with some brown spots), peeled and cut into 1-inch chunks
¼ cup semisweet chocolate chips

EQUIPMENT
Knife
Cutting board
Measuring cups
Medium mixing bowl
Food processor

1 Place the banana chunks in a medium bowl and freeze until solid but not rock-hard (about 30 minutes). You can do this step ahead of time; just let the bananas sit at room temperature for 10 minutes or so before pureeing.

2 Place the banana chunks into a food processor. Process on high (it will be LOUD) until the bananas are a creamy puree.

3 Stir in the chocolate chips and eat right away!

SLIMEY'S SUGGESTION!
Try a tropical soft serve by omitting the chocolate chips and topping the banana puree with toasted coconut and sliced berries, pineapple, or mango!

Cookie Monster's
OATMEAL CRANBERRY BARS
Makes 16 2-inch squares

The tart red cranberries give these bars a festive look, making them perfect for serving at a holiday party or cookie exchange.

INGREDIENTS
½ cup (1 stick) margarine or unsalted butter,
    softened, plus more for greasing pan
½ cup firmly packed light-brown sugar
¼ cup granulated sugar
1 egg
½ teaspoon vanilla
¾ cups all-purpose flour
½ teaspoon baking soda
½ teaspoon cinnamon
¼ teaspoon salt
1½ cups old-fashioned rolled oats
½ cup dried cranberries

EQUIPMENT
Measuring cups
Measuring spoons
Square cake pan (8 x 8-inch)
Large mixing bowl
Small mixing bowl
Whisk
Electric mixer
Wooden spoon

1   Preheat the oven to 350°F. Grease an 8 x 8-inch square cake pan.

2   In a large bowl, with an electric mixer on medium speed, cream the margarine or butter and sugars. Add the egg and vanilla; beat well.

3   In a small bowl, whisk together the flour, baking soda, cinnamon, and salt; with a wooden spoon, stir the dry ingredients into the wet ingredients until well combined. Mix in the oats and cranberries until evenly blended.

4   Spread or press the batter into the cake pan in an even layer. Bake for about 30 minutes or until golden brown. Cool, then cut into 2-inch bars.

Me love dried cranberries!

119

Julia's
BOING-BOING BALLS
Makes about 2 dozen cookies

These melt-in-your-mouth treats are classic holiday cookies. Sometimes called Mexican wedding cakes or Russian tea cakes, they're easy to make and even easier to eat.

INGREDIENTS
Cooking spray, for greasing
½ cup (1 stick) unsalted butter, at room temperature
2 cups confectioners' sugar, divided
2 teaspoons vanilla extract
2 cups all-purpose flour
¼ teaspoon baking powder
1 cup chopped pecans

EQUIPMENT
Measuring cups
Measuring spoons
2 baking sheets
Large mixing bowl
Medium mixing bowl
Electric mixer
Wooden spoon
Medium shallow bowl
Cooling racks

1   Preheat the oven to 300°F. Grease the two baking sheets with the cooking spray.

2   In a large bowl, with an electric mixer on medium speed, cream the butter, ½ cup of the sugar, and the vanilla. In a medium bowl, mix together the flour and baking powder. Add to the butter mixture, stir to mix, then beat until well blended. Stir in the pecans with a wooden spoon.

3   Shape the dough into 1-inch balls and place them about 1 inch apart on the greased baking sheets. Bake until the cookies are a pale golden brown, about 25 minutes. If baking two sheets at once in one oven, switch their positions halfway through baking. Let the cookies stand on the sheets until cool enough to handle, but still warm.

4   Place the remaining 1½ cups of confectioners' sugar in a shallow bowl. Roll the warm cookies in the sugar to coat all over. Set cookies on racks to cool completely.

SLIMEY'S SUGGESTION!
These cookies are egg-free, so a good choice for those with an egg allergy.

Twiddlebug Tip

Make sure the cookies are cool enough to handle before rolling them in the confectioners' sugar. For a chocolate version, mix a little bit of unsweetened cocoa powder in with the confectioners' sugar.

Boing-boing!

Together Time

Cooking and eating together should be fun! The finished food may be delicious, but the time you spend with each other is the most important thing. Here are some ideas for making cooking and mealtime even more magical.

Mix It Up!

MAKING YOUR OWN RECIPES: Kids will be excited to learn that it's easy to customize their own recipes. All you have to do is experiment with the ones in this book! Simple ways to adapt and reimagine recipes include:

- Adding different ingredients to a smoothie! Smoothies taste great with all kinds of additions. Try using frozen fruits that might not be in season or grow where you live—like berries in the winter, or tropical fruits. Throw in a handful of nuts! Use milk or nut and seed butters to make your smoothie creamy, or try using your favorite kind of 100 percent fruit juice to add even more flavor.

- Playing with how fruits and veggies are cut, either for recipes or for snacking. Instead of cutting carrots into sticks, use a vegetable peeler to create long carrot ribbons. Instead of slicing peppers lengthwise, try removing the stem and then cutting circles. If you can find an apple corer, remove the core and then slice apples into rings: presto, "apple doughnuts"! Bananas can be cut into circles or into long slices lengthwise. Oranges can be peeled and then cut into circles. The possibilities are endless!

- Trying new seasonings. Adding a little cinnamon or vanilla extract to a sweet dish changes the flavor. Or try different spices. What would happen if you added a little bit of curry powder to Elmo's Red Lentil Soup (see p. 86)? What kinds of herbs could you try on top of Snuffy's Puffy Focaccia Bread (see p. 66)? If you squeeze a lemon onto a savory dish—like soup, pasta, or chili—the tartness can make the flavors come to life in new and different ways. Give it a try!

- Using different sweeteners. Experiment with brown sugar instead of granulated sugar, or leave out the sugar altogether and use a natural sweetener like honey or maple syrup.

Once you have your new recipe, come up with a fun name for it! Consider writing down any additions or changes in a family recipe book you make yourself. That way you'll remember all your new family recipes!

Play with Your Food!

GAMES TO PLAY WHILE YOU COOK TOGETHER: As you're preparing ingredients or waiting for food to come out of the oven, you'll find there are lots of ways to keep the fun going with kids. Here are a few tips!

- Make cool designs with your food scraps before tossing them away. Carrot peelings, onion skins, melon rinds, and fruit and vegetable odds and ends all have interesting textures and shapes. Try to make symmetrical patterns, create landscapes, or make faces!
- Fill a jar with dried beans. Can you guess how many there are inside? Take them out and group them into sets of 10, then count how many you have in total. You can also

play a game by filling a 1-cup measuring cup with different ingredients—slices of zucchini, pieces of apple, almonds, berries—and guess how many there are.
- When baking, you might have some leftover flour. Dust some over a cutting board or countertop, and let children draw pictures with their fingertips. They'll enjoy the sensation, and you can work on shapes together.

What's your favorite food?

The kind I share with you!

Mealtime Fun!

ENJOYING YOUR TIME AT THE TABLE: Mealtime is a great opportunity to get closer as a family. Ask each other questions, play word games, and talk about your day. Here are some other ideas:

- Conversation starters—get talking with some easy prompts:
  » Make a question jar that you keep filled with slips of paper that have questions such as, "If you could go anywhere in the world, where would it be?" "What superpower would you most like to have?" "If you could have any animal for a pet, what would it be?" Everyone picks a piece of paper, and the whole table gets to answer the questions.
  » Play Roses and Thorns—sometimes called Peaks and Valleys. Ask each person to talk about their best moment of the day and their biggest challenge. Grown-ups can try it, too!

- Food vocabulary game—describe one of the things on your plate. Use words to talk about the way it looks, feels, and tastes. If your child is having trouble coming up with ideas, get the game started for them. For example, "The salad looks colorful, the dressing tastes tangy, and the carrots feel crunchy."
- Explore your plate—sometimes kids need a little encouragement to try new things. To get kids excited about the colorful vegetables on their plates, try inviting them to see which vegetables are crunchy, which are soft, which are smooth, which are tangy, and so on. Or try the "eat your colors" game to see if everyone can find all the colors on their plates and get at least one bite of every color before the meal is over.

Clean It Up!

GIVING KIDS A WAY TO HELP: Kids love responsibility, especially grown-up jobs. So invite kids to join you in cleaning up. Along the way, they'll learn that tidying up is as much a part of the process as the preparation and cooking itself. Kids love wiping down and scrubbing counters, getting dishes nice and sudsy in a sink with warm water and soap, helping to sweep and mop the floor, and putting away ingredients and equipment. Show them where things go the first few times, or tape little pictures onto your cupboards to help them learn. Soon they will be a real help to you in the kitchen at cleanup time!

Index

Image Credits

IS: iStock; MS: Micah Schmidt; SS: Shutterstock